Saving Lake Winnipeg

SAVING LAKE WINNIPEG

ROBERT WILLIAM SANDFORD

RMB

For Alex Salki and Catherine O'Neill Salki,
to whom Canada owes a great debt
for their lifelong commitment to
protecting Lake Winnipeg

❧❧❧❧❧

*Some people change their ways when they see the
light, others when they feel the heat.*

— CAROLYN SCHROEDER

Copyright © 2013 Robert William Sandford

Rocky Mountain Books
www.rmbooks.com

Library and Archives Canada Cataloguing in Publication

Sandford, Robert W., author
    Saving Lake Winnipeg / Robert William Sandford.

(RMB manifesto series)
Includes bibliographical references.
Issued in print and electronic formats.
ISBN 978-1-927330-86-9 (bound).—ISBN 978-1-927330-87-6 (html).—ISBN 978-1-927330-88-3 (pdf)

    1. Winnipeg, Lake (Man.)—Environmental conditions. 2. Cyanobacteria—Manitoba—Winnipeg, Lake. 3. Lake ecology—Manitoba—Winnipeg, Lake. 4. Pollution—Manitoba—Winnipeg, Lake. I. Title. II. Series: RMB manifesto series

QH541.5.L3 S25 2013   577.63'0971272   C2013-903123-5
C2013-903124-3

Printed in Canada

Rocky Mountain Books acknowledges the financial support for its publishing program from the Government of Canada through the Canada Book Fund (CBF) and the Canada Council for the Arts, and from the province of British Columbia through the British Columbia Arts Council and the Book Publishing Tax Credit.

 Canadian Heritage Patrimoine canadien   Canada Council for the Arts Conseil des Arts du Canada

 BRITISH COLUMBIA ARTS COUNCIL
Supported by the Province of British Columbia

The interior pages of this book have been produced on 100% post-consumer recycled paper, processed chlorine free and printed with vegetable-based dyes.

 FSC MIX Paper from responsible sources FSC® C016245

Contents

Lake Winnipeg is dying and we are having trouble figuring out exactly what to do about that. Federal governments in both Canada and the US view the situation as a matter that needs to be addressed at provincial and state levels. Provincial and state governments largely view the problem only from the perspective of their own jurisdictions. Meanwhile the trouble is being compounded by rapid hydro-climatic change that is exacerbating ecological changes that were the source of the problem in the first place. The situation is getting away on us. It has become so increasingly complex that it is difficult to see the larger picture and appreciate its implications, let alone arrive at solutions. This book aims to help the reader understand the expanded context and consequences of the problem we have created for ourselves at the centre of our continent – the problem symbolized by Lake Winnipeg – so that we can collectively summon the means to address this worsening environmental situation.

The current circumstances surrounding the deteriorating condition of Lake Winnipeg and other bodies of water on the Great Plains were perhaps most succinctly characterized at the first-ever joint congress of the Canadian Geophysical Union, the Canadian Water Resources Association and the Canadian Meteorological and Oceanographic Society held in Saskatoon, Saskatchewan, in May 2013. Attended by more than 700 scientists, this week-long sharing of the latest breakthroughs in the earth sciences focused on the bridging of environmental science, policy and resource management. The Lake Winnipeg problem was high on the agenda. The author was invited by Jim Bruce, an organizer of the event and a fellow member of the Forum on Leadership on Water, to summarize the proceedings of a high-level panel discussion on why Lake Winnipeg is dying and why Canadians are failing so badly in preventing that death.

The thoughtful and highly informed conversation spoke very directly to the theme of the congress. A former Manitoba deputy minister of water stewardship, Norm Brandson, outlined the history and character of the problem Canadians have created for themselves with respect to the contamination of Lake Winnipeg.

Jim Bruce, a former deputy minister of Environment Canada, offered lessons that can learned from Lake Erie that might be applied to the accelerated deterioration of the Lake Winnipeg system that may result climate warming.

Ute Holweger and Jason Vanrobaeys of Agriculture and Agri-food Canada discussed management practices that will be required to minimize the runoff of excess fertilizer and manure in the basin.

Water policy experts Robert Halliday and Ralph Pentland then troubled the audience with their concerns related to the loss of federal government science capacity and the decline of federal involvement in matters of urgent environmental concern. Halliday and Pentland balanced these concerns, however, with thoughtful analysis of the economic tools and remaining institutional and legislative capacity that can be brought to bear on the Lake Winnipeg problem.

Mike Renouf of Environment Canada and Ted Yuzyk of the International Joint Commission concluded the panel presentations by demonstrating the role the IJC is playing in bringing Canada and the United States together in a manner that could yield tangible results in addressing not just the Lake Winnipeg problem but the larger issue of the contamination of lakes and streams throughout the Great Plains region.

In order to optimize the value of these leading experts' contributions to understanding the Lake Winnipeg problem, and make the work comprehensible to the average Canadian, the summary of the proceedings was organized around the theme "The Basin We Had, the Basin We Have and the Basin We Want." The basin we had, obviously, is the one that existed in the past. The basin we have is the situation we face today. And of course, the basin we want is its future state, which, as we will see, is very much complicated by the fact that if we don't act decisively now, we may not have much choice about the kind of basin we get.

The basin we had

Norm Brandson described very well the basin we had. What we are dealing with are the remnants of a huge body of water, called Lake Agassiz, which formed 12,000 years ago with the melting of the ice of the last great continental ice age. Lake Agassiz was enormous. At its maximum extent it covered some 500,000 square kilometres. When its water finally burst loose from its glacial confines the volume of release was so great it reshaped the continent and even affected the behaviour of ocean currents. Lake Winnipeg as we know it today is but a vestige of Lake Agassiz.

Before Europeans and other settlers from elsewhere arrived on the scene, Aboriginal people had already been occupying the shores of Lake Winnipeg for more than 8,000 years. Though they are often ignored, the descendants of these people are still there, living in 30 communities in 11 First Nations around the lake.

While only a fraction of the size of Lake Agassiz, Lake Winnipeg is still a very large body of water. At 25,414 square kilometres, it is the tenth-largest freshwater body in the world and the third-largest lake in Canada. It is comprised of two distinct basins: a shallow, turbid southern basin about 100 kilometres long; and a deeper, northern basin 250 kilometres long in which the water is relatively clear. The area of the contributing basin is 40 times the area of the lake surface, which is a surprisingly high ratio for such a large lake.

But this is a lake that cannot escape its past. There is a lot of unresolved history associated with Lake Winnipeg. It is eerie to note, for example, that the lake is slowly moving south in response to isostatic rebound. In the absence of the weight of glacier ice, the land is slowly aspiring to an earlier topography through uplift. The whole basin, however, remembers that it was once a lake bed. The ghost of Lake Agassiz continues to haunt the Central Great Plains. If it could, that ghost would restore Lake Agassiz to its former grandeur, a recurring nightmare that threatens to bankrupt flood-prone jurisdictions like Manitoba.

It is important to note also that because of the presence of phosphorus-rich soil throughout its catchment area, Lake Winnipeg was somewhat contaminated even in its natural state. It could be said that our contemporary efforts to protect the health of the lake are complicated in part by the fact that the lake we had was already fragile and highly vulnerable to the kinds of human activity that created the basin we now have.

The basin we have

The Lake Winnipeg basin drains four Canadian provinces and four US states. Some 800,000 square kilometres of it lies in Canada, and 180,000 square kilometres is in the United States. Three watersheds contribute 90 per cent of the inflow into Lake Winnipeg. Some 43 per cent comes from the Winnipeg River; 32 per cent from the Saskatchewan; and only 10 per cent from the Red and Assiniboine rivers. As we will see later, however, a disproportionate volume of the contaminants entering Lake Winnipeg comes from the sources that contribute the least inflow.

The basin population comprises six million people and 20 million head of livestock. One of these populations has sewage treatment; the other, well, not so much. There are now 23,000 people living permanently on the shores of the lake, and some 10,000 cottages have been built there with a total value estimated at $750-million. Some 600,000 people visit Lake Winnipeg each year to enjoy its beaches. At the moment at least, the lake also supports a vibrant walleye fishery.

The levels of Lake Winnipeg are now regulated. While not widely recognized as such, Lake Winnipeg is now considered one of the largest hydropower reservoirs in the world. Lake level regulation, however, may be causing retention of phosphorus and other contaminants in the lake sediments.

Until about 1970, natural factors were important in driving changes in the basin. Since then, though, land-use impacts and climate change have increased to the point that they almost overshadow natural forces affecting the basin. These trends are expected to accelerate. Unfortunately, there has been a 70 per cent increase in what has been called "nutrient loading" in the lake system over the past 40 years. As a result of these inputs, blue-green algae have flourished in Lake Winnipeg. Algal blooms of up to 15,000 square kilometres are no longer uncommon. Algal toxins are a known danger to humans and animals.

The concentration of phosphorus in overland

flows and in floods has increased dramatically. While phosphorus loading from the South Saskatchewan is likely to decline in future, discharge and loading from the Red and Winnipeg rivers is likely to increase without remedial action. Though it and the Assiniboine contribute only 10 per cent of the inflows into Lake Winnipeg, the American portion of the Red River appears to contribute more than a third of the nutrient load.

Despite investment in the Lake Winnipeg Research Consortium, no comprehensive science program is in place for the entire basin. Comparing the manner in which lakes facing similar deterioration were restored to their original condition in Europe is only marginally helpful because of the much greater relative size of Lake Winnipeg. While lakes 226, 261, 303 and 304 in the Experimental Lakes Area in Ontario offer helpful insights into how to reverse the deteriorating condition of Lake Winnipeg, research efforts remain minuscule compared to the Great Lakes. Based on the comparative number of research papers published on both lakes, it could be said that we know about 25 times more about Lake Erie than we do about Lake Winnipeg.

Similarities between Lake Winnipeg and Lake Erie, however, are worth noting.

Though the drainage areas relative to lake size are very different, Lake Winnipeg and Lake Erie are almost the same length and depth and have nearly the same surface area. The history of the trophic state of Lake Erie is highly instructive. In the 1960s and early 1970s the lake became eutrophic, which is to say that it suffered from excessive algal growth and subsequent oxygen loss in bottom waters in late summer. Some $5-billion was invested through the 1972 Great Lakes Water Quality Agreement to address point source pollution from municipalities and industries. But now Lake Erie is backsliding as a result of increasing sources of diffuse contamination and the effects of climate change. Algal blooms in Lake Erie are now said to be worse than they were in the 1960s, before the first cleanup began, when the lake was thought to be dying.

Additional threats to the health of Lake Erie, such as from invasive species, are now beginning to make their appearance in Lake Winnipeg as well. While regulation of ballast water from ocean-going vessels entering the Great Lakes system appears to have halted the introduction of new species, there are at least 158 lakes in Ontario alone that have been colonized by invasives that originated in the Great Lakes. Rainbow smelt and zebra mussels have made their way into the Lake Winnipeg basin. Under all of these combined threats, Lake Winnipeg may not die, but it could lose much of its life force.

When we think in these ways about what actually exists in the basin we have, as opposed to the one we had, it is impossible not to recognize that the net result of more than a century of water- and land-related policy is the serious degradation and destruction of our country's ecological heritage. If we want the Lake Winnipeg basin to still be a desirable place to live in the future we have to recognize that we are poorer and less healthy as a consequence of managing water badly. Before we discuss the basin we want, however, it is important to point out that such a basin may not be available to us any longer even if we do act decisively now. Before we imagine the world in which we would like to live in the future, it may be necessary to examine first the world we may be forced to accept.

With each 1°C temperature increase we should expect our planet's atmosphere to hold up to 7 per cent more water vapour. Atmospheric water vapour is often referred to as precipitable water. This increase in precipitable water may not result in more total precipitation, but it will result in heavier rains and more extreme rainfall events. The frequency of heavy rain days has already risen from 13 per cent to 27 per cent in the Red River basin. These are runoff-producing rains that wash nutrients in the form of fertilizer and bacteria, E. coli and toxic contaminants from agricultural and urban lands into waterways. As researchers such as the University of Saskatchewan's John Pomeroy and his colleagues have been able to demonstrate, longer, heavier rains have the capacity to increase the mobilization of fecal E. coli on the land by thousands of times. Such runoff is responsible for two-thirds of all water-borne disease outbreaks in North America.

It has also been discovered that continuous greenhouse forcing is strengthening the low-level jet stream which brings moist air from the Gulf of Mexico to the Central Great Plains. This, along with increases in the flow of the Red River, suggests that floods of the magnitude the region has experienced in the last 15 years are likely to become more common in the future. Lake Winnipeg is also warming, which has decreased the period of time during which it is covered by ice, which increases the potential for additional evaporation. This warming is also likely to accelerate already advancing eutrophication. While Lake Winnipeg's thriving walleye fishery has never been better, once eutrophication crosses a tipping point, this fishery could collapse.

The condition of Lake Winnipeg is being noticed abroad. Early in 2013 the Global Nature Fund recognized Lake Winnipeg as the world's "Threatened Lake of the Year." The judges were evidently of the opinion that the enormous area of algal blooms appearing annually and the rate of change in the condition of the lake were unparalleled anywhere else in the world. While this designation certainly made an impression on Manitobans, the fact remains that what is happening to Lake Winnipeg is a symptom of a much larger problem that is beginning to present itself all across Canada and throughout the United States. The eutrophication of streams, rivers and lakes is becoming a much more widespread problem than generally thought. Algal toxins have been detected in nearly 250 lakes across Canada at levels exceeding maximum guidelines in every province. There is every reason to believe that the algal blooms and the carcinogenic toxins they produce will become ever more present in Canadian lakes as water temperatures generally rise and as agricultural production continues to be ramped up to meet growing global food demand. And this is not just a Canadian problem. Eutrophication of freshwater systems as a result of inappropriate agricultural practices has been identified as one of the ten most serious challenges all of humanity faces in the 21st century.

Unpleasant as it is to have been recognized in such a manner, the Global Nature Fund designation could benefit efforts to restore Lake Winnipeg in that it could elevate the larger Central Great Plains issue to one of "urgent national concern," thereby triggering Part 11 of the Canada Water Act. This would make a range of management tools available including loans, grants, effluent discharge fees, fines and compensation. This is good news if only because it tells us that, if enforced, existing laws can be part of the solution, especially if they are employed as part of the suite of economic and institutional considerations that will in tandem be necessary to solve the Lake Winnipeg problem. With all of these considerations on the table, we can now talk about the basin we want.

The basin we want

The basin we know we want is one in which we learn from others who know the problem well and from others who have faced similar problems before us. To do that, however, we have to stop undermining our scientific and policy-making capacity. Ralph Pentland has argued that our national capacity to address environmental concerns has declined by at least a third since 1990. Robert Halliday has expressed the concern that the intellectual and experiential capacity required at all levels to address the Lake Winnipeg problem may no longer exist. Pentland and Halliday argue that we have to stop negotiating national environmental standards into being only to negotiate them away again with no firm commitment of provincial enforcement and follow-up. The Lake Winnipeg problem cannot be addressed without strengthening the hand of government, and in this, science has to be seen as an indispensable tool. But as Mike Renouf of Environment Canada has pointed out, it is very important that we do not focus unduly on Lake Winnipeg alone. The only way Lake Winnipeg will be saved is if we focus on the accurate characterization of the larger regional problem.

Significant gaps exist in our knowledge concerning the effects of the kind of agriculture we are practising, not just in the Lake Winnipeg basin but throughout the Central Great Plains and beyond. This needs serious attention. We need to fill these knowledge gaps, and modelling will help in this. We also need to know and apply the most cost-effective, scientifically proven solutions and then develop decision-support tools that facilitate the implementation of those solutions.

We also have to recognize that we already have institutions like the International Joint Commission, which has been working very successfully on the resolution of transboundary water issues for more than a century. The IJC exists to make cooperation between Canada and the United States over water matters not only possible but highly productive. We have to revitalize and then take full advantage of existing institutions like the IJC if we want to save Lake Winnipeg. We also have to recognize the consequences of failing to do so. It would not be unreasonable to ask – as Ralph Pentland has – what Canada would be like if we had to spend 30 to 40 per cent of our GDP fixing the mistakes of the past.

Economic instruments such as taxes and tradable allowances can play an important role in addressing the problems that are emerging on the Central Great Plains, but only if these measures are supported by appropriate legislation and regulation that is effectively and consistently enforced.

To bring into existence the basin we want by restoring Lake Winnipeg to health we have to:

℧ reduce high spring flows of the Red River;
℧ reduce the concentration of phosphorus available for mobilization on the land throughout the Red River basin;

- strengthen the hand of government in a non-partisan way so as to allow the creation of regulatory regimes that will give all sectors of the economy clear direction and incentives to operate appropriately and effectively in service of addressing the larger Central Great Plains flooding and eutrophication problem;
- require the implementation of beneficial management practices in all sectors currently contributing to the larger Lake Winnipeg problem; and
- support efforts to slow rates of climate change by reducing greenhouse emissions in North America and globally.

Continuing support for programs such as the "Lake Friendly" initiative and the harvesting of biomass from Lake Winnipeg's inlet marsh to produce bio-energy as proposed by the International Institute for Sustainable Development will be vital to success. Since nearly half of the phosphorus flowing into Lake Winnipeg originates from the US part of the Red River basin, action in the US through the International Joint Commission's Red River

Board must also be vigorously pursued. Examples of how international cooperation can be made to yield mutually beneficial outcomes can be found in the Great Lakes Basin and in the Netherlands. The mechanisms the Ontario Ministry of the Environment now uses to regulate phosphorus discharges into the South Nation River can also be instructive.

It is important to point out, however, that a non-binding Lake Winnipeg Accord such as has been put forward by the Manitoba government may not accurately frame the wider extent of the problem and may not adequately engage our American neighbours. What is needed is an agreement that presses governments at all levels and every sector of the economy into direct, measurable service of the goal of restoring eco-hydro-climatic stability to the Central Great Plains region. What may be required is nothing less than an international Great Plains Agreement similar to what was agreed upon by Canada and the United States to jointly manage the Great Lakes.

A week after the combined congress of the Canadian Geophysical Union, the Canadian

Meteorological and Oceanographic Society and the Canadian Water Resources Association in Saskatoon in May 2013, Manitoba's Minister of Conservation and Water Stewardship, the Hon. Gordon Mackintosh, announced a newly expanded plan to address the larger Lake Winnipeg problem through what will be called the Lake Friendly Accord and Stewardship Alliance. The alliance will be made up of more than 40 key stakeholder organizations having a critical role in the health of Lake Winnipeg. This will include representation from governments, conservation districts, the agricultural sector, Aboriginal communities, business groups and environmental organizations. The Lake Friendly Accord builds on the successful Lake Friendly web-based program to engage all sectors of society in a common goal of improving water quality across the Lake Winnipeg basin. It will focus on facilitation, information sharing, enhanced collaboration and co-ordination, improved reporting and accountability and the prioritization of science-based provincial action on the larger Lake Winnipeg problem. While it does not assure formal co-operation between federal governments or the

Canadian provinces and US states that share the Lake Winnipeg basin, this announcement makes it clear that the government of Manitoba is taking the problem seriously.

Whether or not even a committed provincial government can succeed in such an endeavour remains unclear. At the time of this writing the federal government was in the process of abandoning top-down responsibility for matters related to the environment. Its claim that its role is to steer while the provinces row won't allow anyone to arrive at a solution to the larger Lake Winnipeg problem. The federal governments in both countries must play an active role in creating this process and sustaining the integration that will make it successful. Only a highly mobilized top-down and bottom-up process will stimulate the kind of nested watershed approach that is needed if we are to address the extent of hydro-climatic change we presently face on the Central Great Plains.

So we arrive back at the question that remains at the heart of the Lake Winnipeg situation: Can we build a bridge between environmental science, effective public policy and sustainable resource management? Such a bridge has clearly existed for some time in Canada, but it remains incomplete. There remains, however, room for optimism. Robert Halliday and Ralph Pentland certainly made room for hope in their closing remarks at the Saskatoon congress: "Is it too late to save Lake Winnipeg? Absolutely not."

We saved Lake Erie once; surely we can do it again. If the same remedial actions now being implemented to revive the ecological dead zone at the mouth of the Mississippi on the Gulf of Mexico were extended to the Red River Basin, "nutrient" flows into Lake Winnipeg could be greatly reduced. To save Lake Winnipeg, however, we may – all of us – have to recognize the larger problem we need to address if we wish to do so and not just concentrate on the specific economic, environmental and social issues that concern us individually. Through collaboration and coop- eration the health of Lake Winnipeg and the eco- logical and agricultural integrity of the Central Great Plains can be restored. Accomplishing that goal is what this book is about.

Some Climate Context

Given there are so many voices who are paid to deny the existence of climate change or to confuse the public about its implications, it is important that anyone who speaks publicly on such issues clearly declare their biases from the outset so that their interests are transparent and cannot be misunderstood or misinterpreted. Though I have a science background, I am not a scientist. I do, however, work in the scientific community. My role there is to translate research outcomes into language the average person can understand and that decision-makers in both government and the private sector can use to craft timely and durable public policy. So, if scientific method be a bias, let me clearly declare mine.

There is strong evidence that our climate is an emergent property of an interconnected, telekinetic global system. I trust this evidence. And this same evidence confirms that our atmosphere is a product of continuous interaction between land, life, water, air and sunlight. Recent research clearly demonstrates we have been underestimating life's role in determining and regulating the composition of our atmosphere, not only throughout past geological ages but also and particularly in our own time. The body of knowledge to which I am constantly exposed indicates that the physical functions of global climate are in fact being altered by influences associated with changes in the composition and character of terrestrial ecosystems, brought about by human influences on land use, which are then accelerated by wholesale, large-scale addition of by-products of human energy use that are in turn rapidly changing the composition of the earth's atmosphere.

There is further evidence, which I also trust, that the risks posed by the combination of natural ecosystem decline and climate change are real and tangible and threaten the planetary life-support system upon which humanity depends for its stability and sustainability. I also hold these risks to be serious enough to require constantly improving forms of human intervention and management. After decades of weighing the science, I am now of the opinion that we would be wise to minimize these risks by reducing the vulnerability of those exposed to them, by restoring lost ecological and hydrological function, and by minimizing further changes to the composition of our planet's atmosphere.

After scientific examination of the wide range of observed and projected hydro-climatic effects, especially those related to what the insurance industry has determined are increases in the frequency, intensity and duration of highly damaging extreme weather events, it is now widely held that the loss of hydro-climatic stability can no longer be characterized simply as an environmental problem. Nor is it accepted that climate change is a problem that can be solved simply by the further application of engineering innovation or finesse. Rising mean atmospheric temperatures are quickly becoming social, economic and political issues, both nationally and globally. Decades of following the science has convinced me that climate change is an emerging condition under which human beings will have to make choices about how we govern ourselves. When I speak of governance, what I am talking about are the principles and standards by which we allow our collective affairs to be managed. What I am talking about are our collective values.

It is important, however, not to overreact to the loss of hydro-climatic stability. This is not the end of the world; we have the capacity collectively to address global climate-related concerns. But I would feel considerably more optimistic about the future if public discourse over climate change were more honest and principled and possessed greater intellectual rigour. I would have more confidence in the future if our provincial and federal governments would take climate change more seriously. I would feel a great deal more hopeful if we had a coherent vision of the kind of country we would like to have and create in the face of so much change. I could perhaps be induced to feel cautiously optimistic about the future if that vision had its roots where I live in the upland watersheds of Canada's western mountains. Unfortunately, at the time of this writing it is difficult to feel much optimism. In fact, I feel that the amount of time we as a society have wasted in dithering over whether and how we should address this problem could cost us much of what we count on today to give our lives meaning and value. It is the purpose of this book to change that. I believe we can, as a society, deal with these problems, but to do so we first have to fully recognize them for what they are and for how serious they have become. Failure to do this would equate to what some historians have called a March of Folly.

Defining the March of Folly

The meeting was held at Simon Fraser University's downtown campus, in the very heart of Vancouver's business district. There were 24 people in the room, each representing a different sector of the economy, level of government or academic department. Despite wide differences in background, everyone at the meeting was interested in how they could best orchestrate their own ability to adapt over time to changing climatic conditions and their consequences. The discussions over the course of the day were largely about risk. A senior policy-maker for one of the world's largest insurance companies stole the show early in the day with a presentation on how insurers are viewing the climate change threat.

Lindene Patton of Zurich Financial Services began her presentation by graphically illustrating how aggregating and increasing losses due to extreme weather events around the world are changing the way insurance companies use rate adjustment to incentivize risk reduction. She noted that fewer people are buying insurance in high-risk areas, trusting governments instead to rescue them financially in the event of recurring floods, hurricanes and other disasters. She also noted that in places such as Florida, recurring natural calamities are putting the cost of disaster relief out of reach even for governments. She pointed out that there was a very great difference between insured and uninsured losses, and that the capacity of governments to cover these risks and losses is diminishing everywhere. Patton concluded her comments by observing that, as a consequence of growing understanding of the risks, precedents in tort liability in the United States are suggesting that it may not be long before legal action can be brought against politicians who bring about harm to others, or to others' property, as a result of decisions that wilfully ignore potential climate change impacts.

A retired former deputy minister of environment for British Columbia, Jon O'Riordan, was invited to summarize the discussion that followed Patton's and other presentations which took up the rest of the day. O'Riordan articulated our current situation with respect to climate change in Canada in an unexpected way. Borrowing the title of a bestselling 1984 book by celebrated American historian Barbara Tuchman, O'Riordan characterized our country's failure to act on the climate change threat as our nation's March of Folly.

Tuchman, O'Riordan explained, had observed throughout history a recurring pattern of societies failing to see and act on serious threats to their own stability and future until it was too late to do anything meaningful about them. Tuchman applied very strict historical criteria to determine whether a particular case fit the pattern, and the kinds of misgovernment she observed usually occurred as a result of one or a combination of four leadership flaws. These include tyranny or oppression; excessive ambition; incompetence or decadence; and folly or perversity.

To qualify under the special category of folly or perversity, choices made by leaders had to meet three further criteria. First, they must be perceived as counterproductive in their own time, not merely in hindsight. Tuchman is firm on this. It is unfair to judge choices made in the past by the ideas and values of the present. Leadership directions can only be judged as folly and perversity if they were perceived in their own time as wrongheaded even as they were being established and implemented. The second criterion for judging leadership direction as mere folly was that a feasible alternative course of action must have been available. Finally, in order to ensure that history is not unfairly attributing the blame to individual leaders, the third criterion was that the policy direction in question should be one that was formulated by more than just one leader, and should persist beyond the lifetime of any given politician or term of office of any given political party. When these criteria are added together the picture of folly emerges. Folly or perversity is the pursuit of policies that are contrary to the ultimate self-interest of the constituency or state over generations. "Folly's appearance," Tuchman notes, "is independent of era or locality; it is timeless and universal, although the habits and beliefs of a particular time and place determine the form it takes."

No one, it appears, is immune to such folly. We have observed even in Canada that self-deception is a factor that can play a significant role in the process of governance at national, provincial and municipal levels. It becomes most obvious when it manifests itself in the form of governments assessing situations in terms of preconceived notions and established agendas while rejecting or ignoring contrary signs. Our current situation with respect to the accelerating impacts of land-use change and green house gas emissions on climate change, O'Riordan observed, meets all of Barbara Tuchman's conditions for a full-on, inter-generational failure to see and act upon a serious threat to the stability and future of our society until it is too late to do anything about it but accept the consequences.

We have unwittingly allowed the growth imperative and economic self-interest to dominate the global political agenda at the expense of action on the obvious, clearly recognized decline of planetary life-support system function and the growing effects of climate change on our social and economic well-being. By choosing to base our economy on unsustainable land-use and on agricultural practices and industrial activities that accelerate changes in the composition of our planetary atmosphere, Canada has chosen to become a "superpower" in advancing our global society in this direction. The March of Folly has begun and it has everything to do with the relationship between land, water and climate. Canada has joined that march.

Taking back the truth

From Tuchman's 1984 book, fast forward twenty years to Jared Diamond's bestseller called *Collapse: How Societies Choose To Fail or Succeed* for yet more evidence of our society's fascination with how civilizations can blunder into demise even though they brought it on themselves and clearly saw it coming. If we critically evaluate what we are doing now, we can see how this can happen. With wealth and power concentrated in the right hands, and with the right public relations and advertising campaign and an indifferent public, millions of people will unwittingly become part of a March of Folly they didn't know they joined. Stimulated by the right rhetoric and appropriately stirring music, whole societies will march like lemmings right off the cliff into disaster.

It was these concerns about our society's slowness to respond to the need for effective climate-change adaptation that I took to Dr. John Pomeroy, a Canada Research Chair in hydrology and climate change at the University of Saskatchewan and one of the world's most respected climate scientists. Pomeroy calmly observed that there was a similar public backlash against gloomy climate forecasts in the United Kingdom in the last decade. Scientists responded by soft-pedalling climate change talk in order to prevent the public from blocking out information regarding changes that were already taking place but that people did not want to accept were occurring. He likened the public reaction in the UK to how a diagnosis of a terminal illness is often rejected or ignored rather than faced.

Others, he noted, need the straight story in order to decide how to act.

Dr. Pomeroy thinks many dedicated people working on the climate change problem want to be careful so as to prevent the public from seizing up. This is fine as far as it goes, he offered, but ultimately, soft-pedalling the problem isn't going to change the patient's condition. Nor will the fact that the patient has refused treatment. Pomeroy observed that in the summer of 2012 all of Greenland was melting for the first time since satellite measurements became possible, and that Arctic sea ice extent is at a record low. "We are in serious trouble," he said, "and we need to be honest with ourselves about the threat."

Pomeroy went on to note that science has identified the problem but not the solution. Noting that southwestern Saskatchewan "adapted" to the drought of the 1930s by having three-quarters of its population abandon their farms and leave the region, he observed that adaptation in its own right was not necessarily a solution. Pomeroy called what happened on the Canadian prairies during the Great Depression giving in or giving up, and unfortunately that may be the sum total of the options people will be left with as land-use impacts and increasing emissions accelerate the effects of climate warming. Some regions may again have to be abandoned. In this context, he said, adaptation can start out being clever but in the end may be brutal beyond imagining. By not addressing this problem seriously now, Pomeroy concluded, our weak political leadership in Canada is laying the foundation for an inevitable phase in which adaptation will be not a pleasant option but a harsh necessity.

I have come to the conclusion that I too fear adaptation, at least as it is being framed at the time of this writing. In its present iteration, adaptation means we wait until something happens here of the magnitude of the recent droughts and floods in Australia, or worse, before we accept that we have to take the climate change threat seriously. After 40 years of working in biological systems I am not deluded about how severe last-minute adaptation can be and how indifferent history is to who wins and who loses. I think of the Permian extinction, which Pomeroy and I discussed when we met. From a public relations point of view, it could be said there indeed was successful adaptation during that time. All told, a whopping 5 per cent of all extant species managed to adapt. Unfortunately, 95 per cent didn't.

We are in the midst of a similar extinction now, though you wouldn't get a sense of that in Canada. As Pomeroy pointed out, we didn't do much better than in the Permian in adapting to drought on the Great Plains in the 1930s, and it doesn't look like we are going to do much better in the entire Central Great Plains region of North America if current climate trends persist there in the coming decades. Historian Donald Worster's prediction (*Dust Bowl*, 1979), that we didn't learn enough about adaptation from the 1930s in that region, could very well prove true.

Across the country we are now talking about "mainstreaming" the adaptation imperative. But in all of the federally supported adaptation initiatives to which I have been exposed, we appear to be completely ignoring the fact that special interests have hijacked public discourse over the climate threat. It is as if we have become wilfully blind to the real problem.

We appear helpless to prevent the muzzling, even silencing, of the physical scientists who are bringing forward incontrovertible evidence of the seriousness of the climate change threat. Many of those concerned about the climate issue are now reduced to timidly begging and wheedling their way into public consciousness through happy talk that focuses on terms like "sustainability" and "resilience," which in the context of their current usage have little meaning in a world where hydro-climatic stability has already been lost. Those genuinely concerned about the climate threat are reduced to walking on eggshells, trying to make sure they don't say anything that will in some way raise the ire of established local or external forces of denial or attract the attention of anyone associated with these forces, no matter how junior their rank. It is only now becoming apparent that, in accepting this as the best approach we can come up with in response to what effectively is tyranny, we are in fact legitimizing in the public imagination the fact that these interests have lied to us, appropriated our language, hijacked public discourse and are stealing our future. If we want to end our March of Folly, this cannot continue.

Ecological, hydrologic and climate systems are already on the move in many parts of Canada.

Parts of some regions – like the Central Great Plains of North America – may soon no longer be desirable for human habitation. Those places that adapt and become more resilient *will* be better off, provided global warming is kept below 2°C. They will be better off at least temporarily unless they are overwhelmed by refugees that didn't or couldn't adapt in the place where they formerly lived.

This migration, as I have been saying for years, will be inland, uphill and toward cooler temperatures and water (IUTW). Canada's mountain West will be one of the places found to be most desirable to people migrating from regions like the US Southwest and Central Great Plains, either as a result of drought or extreme weather and flooding events brought about by higher mean annual atmospheric temperatures.

So what do we do? Criticism of how seriously we are taking the climate threat in Canada will not be one bit useful unless it is followed by a proposal for a better or at least more effective way forward. It appears to me that the most appropriate suite of actions would be to establish a renewed three-prong campaign in support of advancing the adaptation imperative in this country.

Step one: Affirm, trust and communicate the facts, however unpopular they may be

David Suzuki has been relentless in speaking out over land-use impacts and the failure to contain greenhouse emissions that in tandem are accelerating climate change. His profile in fact was so high and he was such an irritant to our federal government that his foundation was one of the first big targets of the Canada Revenue Agency's crackdown on climate change and oil sands dissent funded by not-for-profit foundations.

To my utter amazement, a surprising number of people thought Suzuki had it coming. This in itself demonstrates the effectiveness of the public relations campaign to which the Canadian public has been quietly subjected. If we want to break up the March of Folly, we cannot write off people like David Suzuki as examples we can no longer follow simply because he had the courage and conviction to speak out, especially given that so few others were prepared to do as he did. If Canadians gave deeper thought to what is happening, we would rise up as a nation against forms of political high-handedness like this that threaten our fundamental freedom of speech and association, which happen to be at the heart of what it means to live in a democracy. If we don't as a society care about such rights – at least in the context of the debate we need to have over eco-hydro-climatic change in Canada – we are left with few choices as to how we can take back the truth.

Our first strategy, in my opinion at least, should be to trust legitimate science and to put its findings confidently and persistently before the public. The goal of this strategy is to hammer away boldly every day at profiling what the rising tide of new scientific evidence means to our prospects today and to our security and prosperity tomorrow. This campaign needs to be utterly honest, but it also needs to be as relentless as the disinformation campaign organized by denialist interests. Under this ceaseless barrage of new and relevant facts, progress has to be made as quickly as possible in the advancement of public acceptance of the need for not just ritual but actual steps toward adaptation that really do result in enhanced community and societal resilience. But simply freeing and enabling those who would advance the adaptation agenda is not enough. We have to go after the blockage that is preventing our march from being recognized for the folly it is.

Step two: Aggressively refute disinformation
Many thoughtful people around the world are arguing that we can no longer let climate change deniers, especially in developed countries with disproportionately large greenhouse emissions, off the hook without having to at least explain and justify their opinions and inaction. This is not to say we shouldn't entertain debate on the climate issue. We must continue to debate it vigorously and continuously. We can no more allow advocacy for climate change action to become an unquestionable religion than we can allow deniers simply to dismiss the threat without explanation. But to be productive, the debate cannot continue to be as contaminated as it has been allowed to become in Canada.

When we permit elected officials and other elites to argue that they don't accept scientific evidence for climate change and that they are above explaining their logic, we are allowing deniers to elevate their arguments, without our permission, out of the arena of rational debate and into the moral equivalent of unchallengeable religious convictions. By allowing influential people among us to get away with portraying categorical denial of climate change effects as an unassailable article of faith in this way is to stifle crucial debate and cave in to the basest and most perverse of all public relations manipulations.

Acceptance or rejection of climate change impacts on our world is not a matter of faith. To permit it to be characterized as such is to deny the validity of disciplined research undertaken by thousands of highly trained specialists over more than four decades of careful observations worldwide. These research outcomes have been vetted through the most comprehensive peer review in the history of science. Of nearly 14,000 papers published between 1991 and 2012, only 24 rejected evidence that we have disrupted our global climate. This body of peer-reviewed research clearly indicates that our climate is changing faster than at any other time in at least half a million years and that we humans are the cause of much of it.

Every time we allow our purported leaders in government, business, agriculture or industry to simply dismiss climate change effects because it is more convenient in the short term to ignore them, we permit those who do not want to respond logically to the climate issue to escape both responsibility and meaningful action by making unexamined opinions an acceptable foundation for maintaining an increasingly toxic and unsustainable status quo. To do so is as illogical as allowing people to argue that slavery is acceptable or that is it is reasonable to exterminate an objectionable minority, without demanding to know why.

Again, it is time to take back the truth. History has already proven that narrow-minded points of view artificially elevated beyond reproach can be made to hold great public sway. We already know that careful public-relations manipulation can make it appear that even the most ridiculous opinions no longer need to be consistent with the demands and dictates of scientific logic, first-hand experience or even common sense. We also know that it is at exactly this point that the world suddenly becomes a very dangerous place.

Enough evidence has now been put forward to make it clear that public discourse with respect to climate issues has been polluted for decades by corporately funded disinformation campaigns (see Appendix). It is obvious now to almost everyone who has been paying attention that plain old charlatans have been presented as credible voices to the public on climate matters in which their only interest has been to manufacture doubt. Now that people all over the world are seeing with their own eyes the kinds of storms and floods and droughts which scientists have long predicted would result from warming temperatures, professional deniers and the governments they have infiltrated are left only with smear tactics. The scientific community is at last waking up to the fact that it is engaged in a street fight, over facts that affect our future, in which civility is no longer relevant.

Scientists are now being subjected not just to peer review but to the same kinds of ad hominem attacks once reserved only for politicians. These assaults take the form of lies repeated often enough to be perceived as truth by the public. It is time we recognized that the term "skeptic" has been co-opted to describe those who deny as opposed to those who appraise critically. In the context of the climate debate, this distorted form of skepticism has been adopted and refined as a powerful public relations tactic.

A fact that has been ignored in this undeclared and well-funded public-relations war against climate science is that peer review is what separates fact from fancy and wishful thinking in science. As Michael Mann has pointed out, peer review is in fact legitimate skepticism in practice. While peer review and the demands of the scientific method do not permit practitioners to say anything they can't prove, the liars and bullies waging their war against truth are permitted to say whatever they want, time and again, without having to be accountable for whether or not what they are saying is true. This has to stop. It is time to stand up to the liars for hire who are helping to steal our future.

Taking back the truth means we have to start publicly challenging the credentials, connections, opinions, logic and motives of those who persistently stand in the way of public understanding and political action on land-use and water-related climate matters. We can no longer let those who represent vested interests bring the same tired, irrational and repeatedly disproved short-sighted economic objections forward again and again. We cannot allow such voices to continually have the floor without demanding to know who they are, who they work for and whether their views are based on fact or are just part of the public-relations spin of the army of interests who are occupying our country and representing us in government without our permission.

Only by bringing the war against climate science to a close in Canada will we be able to see clearly what is really possible for us to accomplish in the future. In being honest with ourselves, we may well discover there is a great deal more we can do than we thought, and that the future holds more promise than we ever expected or even imagined.

Step three: Strategies for stopping the March of Folly
We have already wasted 25 years denying eco-hydro-climatic change and its obvious large-scale

effects in regions like the Arctic and the Central Great Plains of North America. It is time to get moving. In tandem with an intensified focus on communicating the growing body of new scientific findings and perspectives that underscore the urgency, efforts have to be made at every turn to vocalize the need to take adaptation seriously. The goal is to make communities not just more resilient but actually sustainable. A further objective would be to avoid the situation that is now emerging on the Central Great Plains where municipalities, provinces, states and federal governments find themselves powerless to both cover the risks and pay for the damage caused by extreme weather events and still have enough money left over to address and adapt to the root causes of that damage so as to reduce vulnerability in the future. Adaptation has to be seen as possible, but that will only happen if we actively make it so.

Though often only at the planning stages of development, the fundamental strategies for ending the March of Folly are actually already solidly embedded in the adaptation initiatives of many communities and regions.

The first strategy is to clearly determine how the intensification of the global hydrological cycle, including rising temperatures and changes in the seasonal timing of snowmelt, will affect local and regional water balances and water supplies. Part of this strategy is to ascertain when geographic regions are most vulnerable and to determine the most effective ways to translate scientific findings into communications that will foster effective stakeholder interaction, policy development and local decision-making.

The second strategy is to determine the extent to which future hydrologic extremes such as droughts and floods may be different in frequency, intensity and duration from those of the present and what the consequences may be for local infrastructure as it has been developed to date. It will be particularly important to recognize the challenges to be faced in situations where stationarity of hydrological regimes and linearity with respect to change may no longer apply. In many municipalities and regions it will be necessary to completely rezone floodplains in response to uncertain, even erratic hydro-climatic trends.

In some areas it may be necessary to imagine and plan for a very different future.

The third strategy is to undertake cross-disciplinary and integrated assessments of how hydro-climatic change will affect relationships between land use, socio-economic systems and ecological processes on a local and regional scale. In many places in Canada, adaptation strategies continue to be developed in ways that focus on the possible linear effects of higher mean atmospheric temperatures on water supply and quality. But when ecological, hydrological and climatic systems start changing in tandem, the result may not be linear. Chain reactions are not out of the question. Step-like changes can occur rapidly as systems cross eco-hydro-climatic thresholds that in many cases were not known to exist until they were crossed. In cases where this happens, the changes may be irreversible, at least within any meaningful human time frame. The reality of these earthly thresholds is seldom taken into account when proposals come forward that suggest it will be possible to geo-engineer our way out of the climate change problem.

Finally, there is an urgent need to develop new visualization materials for effective cross-disciplinary communication that will graphically demonstrate to the public the kinds of creative responses that will be necessary if we are to adjust to non-linear hydro-climatic changes. To be effective and meaningful, such communication must clearly illustrate the link between resilience and sustainability on the one hand and the threat of collapse on the other, for that is the juncture in history at which we unfortunately stand. The first national project we should undertake in our efforts to stop the March of Folly should be an all-out endeavour to save Lake Winnipeg.

A misconception I would like to put to rest is that I have taken up this issue and written this book as an outsider wishing to tell those who live in Manitoba and larger Central Great Plains region what they are doing wrong and what they should do differently. The truth is that I am not an outsider. The fact that I live in Alberta means that I too live in the Lake Winnipeg basin: at the headwaters of the Saskatchewan River system. I am concerned about Lake Winnipeg because I have an uncomfortable feeling that the problems that have begun to present themselves there are already beginning to appear at a theatre very near me. From this perspective this book is not about what *someone else* should or must do, but what *we together* can do to address the eco-hydrological and climate threats that will ultimately face us all.

I have seen first-hand what has happened

elsewhere in the world under similar circumstances and I do not want those things to happen here. I fear that most of the people who live in the Lake Winnipeg basin and the Central Great Plains region have no idea of the seriousness and complexity of the environmental and climate problems we face. There are, however, many who have already recognized this seriousness and complexity and who are doing their best to act on what they know. Before exploring that complexity, it may be useful to put the Lake Winnipeg into a larger context of water issues in Canada.

Wherever I travel in this country, the first question I am invariably asked is whether Canada really does face a water crisis. To many, I'll have to admit, the very notion is ludicrous. "How, in a land in which there is so much water," they ask, "could such a thing even be possible?" Canada is blessed with more fresh water than any other country on the planet, and if you compute it on a per capita basis, with our sparse population, our water wealth reaches stratospheric proportions.

But abundance, in this case, leads to dangerous complacency. Water experts, as opposed to the general public, have been seeing the warning signs for years and have attempted, mostly futilely, to catch the country's attention. They talk of population increases and industrial land uses that put inexorable pressure on the water supply. They warn that surface water in many places is now fully utilized, leaving us dependent on groundwater in the future, without protections in place to save that groundwater from contamination. They point to our aging water infrastructure – pipelines, canals, reservoirs, pumping stations – and predict public health problems for future generations. (Remember Walkerton, Ontario, in 2000?) They are particularly concerned about industrial-scale agriculture and the degradation of water that it causes. There are new contaminants – pharmaceuticals, hormones, endocrine-disrupting compounds – entering the water system every day and not getting filtered out when the water is recycled for reuse. There are also growing concerns about pipeline leaks and the chemicals used in subsurface hydraulic fracturing. And looming over all the experts' warnings is the vast and unpredictable canopy of climate change.

If things stay the same, none of the issues I

have listed need constitute – by itself – anything that could properly be called a national water crisis in Canada. There is one small problem, however. Things are not staying the same. After a century of relative stability, rising atmospheric temperatures have begun to drive changes in the rate and manner in which water is moving through the hydrological cycle. (You remember the hydrological cycle from Grade 9 geography, right? Evaporation → condensation → precipitation etc., etc.) Changes in the hydrological cycle, in tandem with our other water problems, may be the only thing that could actually create a bona fide water crisis in Canada. It is with the discovery of evidence supporting this view that the story of Lake Winnipeg begins. It is a story, however, that doesn't start at Lake Winnipeg itself, but farther north, in the Mackenzie River basin.

Northern waters, southern insights

Over the past decade the people of the Northwest Territories have found themselves confronting hydro-climatic changes they cannot easily adapt to and can no longer ignore. In addition to water quality concerns related to upstream oil sands development, they are seeing rapid loss of permafrost, changes in weather and obvious diminution of snowpack and snowcover.

Collaboration to address such issues began in 2005 and resulted in the publication of "Northern Voices, Northern Waters," the Northwest Territories water stewardship strategy. Water experts from across the country were then asked to comment on the strategy in an 18-city tour sponsored by RBC's Blue Water Project. An utterly unexpected outcome of the national tour was the realization that the same kind of ecological-hydrological-climatic impacts being tracked in the NWT were already affecting many other regions of the country in highly damaging ways that were not being connected with one another or with climate change.

It was not until we were well into the speaking tour and visiting Manitoba that we discovered that here was a region in plain sight in southern Canada that was changing even more rapidly than the Arctic. According to some experts, southern Manitoba in particular appeared to be approaching – or perhaps had even passed over an invisible threshold into – a new hydro-climatic state that residents have been unable to even cope with, let alone adapt to. At first we thought this region could be defined and confined geographically as the Lake Winnipeg basin. As I will demonstrate, we found out later the problem was much more widespread than that.

The Lake Winnipeg basin

The Lake Winnipeg basin occupies one million square kilometres and extends over four Canadian provinces – Alberta, Saskatchewan, Manitoba and part of Ontario – and four American states – Montana, North Dakota, South Dakota and Minnesota – in the Central Great Plains region of North America. The first evidence of problems in the basin was that algal blooms in Lake Winnipeg began to grow in size over the course of each summer. Algal abundance has increased 300 to 500 per cent since 1900.

Algal blooms of up to 15,000 square kilometres have now begun to appear in the lake annually. The presence of so much algae prevents light penetration and oxygen absorption, causing a condition called eutrophication which in extreme cases can limit the amount of oxygen available for other species and thereby reduce biodiversity in a given aquatic ecosystem. Then came the cyanobacteria, a form of blue-green algae that can produce toxins so strong they can sicken and even kill animals and people. Cyanotoxins can also bio-accumulate in fish and shellfish, which then become poisonous if eaten.

Over the last twenty years, it has been scientifically demonstrated that the increased area of algal blooms and growing presence of toxic cyanobacteria in Lake Winnipeg are a warning of larger eco-hydrological problems, not just in the immediate lake area but throughout the region. Combined with the major spring flooding in the basin, which has been setting new records in the past decade, the effects in the Lake Winnipeg basin are proving to be drastic and deadly.

Recent research shows that the spring floods create a wash effect which flushes nitrogen and phosphorus contained in livestock and wildlife feces and agricultural fertilizers from the land surface into Lake Winnipeg. The ultra-high concentrations of these substances form the nutrient supply for the algal blooms. The flooding problem has been made much worse by the draining of up to 90 per cent of the natural wetlands throughout the region to improve agricultural productivity. These wetlands not only stored water in times of flood but also acted as sinks in which nitrogen and phosphorus would concentrate, enabling natural ecosystem function to purify runoff before it poured into Lake Winnipeg. Further climatic influences associated with warming are likely to exacerbate all of these already existing problems.

The situation in the Central Great Plains is so serious that it is no longer being described simply as an environmental problem. It is now seen as a major threat to the economic future of the entire region. There is growing concern that the cost of persistent flooding and related damage will in time be substantial enough to make it difficult to sustain prosperity in this region as we know it today. As pointed out earlier, the risk economically is that the people of the region will not be able to afford to do both: deal with the recurring disasters *and* address the causes of them. Parts of this region are not going to be habitable, and the costs of ongoing flood damage may be of a magnitude that could bankrupt Manitoba. These same effects are of such a scale globally that adaptation is no longer an option but an urgency. So how did this happen and what exactly is going on here that constitutes evidence of a potential water crisis in Canada?

Historical flooding in the region

Because it was once at the bottom of glacial Lake Agassiz, the topography of southern Manitoba resembles the shape of a soup bowl. Every time the region gets a lot of rain, Lake Agassiz tries to reconstitute itself. Sometimes it briefly succeeds. A flood in 1950 caused the evacuation of more than 100,000 people, flooded 10,000 homes in the Winnipeg area and destroyed four of the city's eleven bridges, resulting in total damage of more than $700-million (the equivalent of $7-billion today, according to the Bank of Canada's inflation calculator webpage). In the wake of the 1950 disaster, all levels of government began to implement flood protection programs. Even as the floodwaters were receding, the Greater Winnipeg Dyking Board sought federal government disaster assistance funding for two projects. The first was for a raised boulevard dike fifty kilometres long through the city of Winnipeg. The second was investment in a series of pumping stations that would allow the city's sewers to continue functioning during floods. The disaster also resulted in recommendations in 1958 by the Manitoba Royal Commission on Flood Cost Benefit that included the construction of a detention basin at Sainte-Agathe formed by a forty-kilometre dike across the Red River Valley; a diversion of the Assiniboine River around the town of Portage la Prairie; and a forty-kilometre ditch that would divert flood waters at St. Norbert and return them to the Red River at St. Andrews, allowing flood waters to completely bypass metropolitan Winnipeg. The total cost of these major public works was $100-million, bringing the cost of the 1950 flood to $800-million ($8-billion today).

In 1966 another flood disaster in the Red River valley resulted in the creation of a program that funded further dike expansion and paid farmers to construct elevated earth pads to protect grain bins and other important farm structures. Again the cost was in the millions.

In 1976 the province of Manitoba entered into

Flood Damage Reduction Program Agreements under the Canada Water Act which funded the mapping of flood hazard zones; the upgrading of flood forecasting; the raising of dikes to the once-in-100-years flood level; and the floodproofing of buildings in hazard zones. The cost was in the tens of millions of dollars.

In 1979 there was another flood of the same magnitude as in 1950. Some $7-million was committed to further ring dikes around communities and for additional dike maintenance. New standards required new buildings to be built to the 1979 flood level plus an additional 60 centimetres. Unfortunately these standards did not prove adequate when "the flood of the century" hit southern Manitoba in 1997.

The 1997 flood occurred along the Red River in North Dakota, Minnesota and southern Manitoba in April and May and resulted in the evacuation of 28,000 people and some $500-million in damage in southern Manitoba alone. While cities like Fargo and Winnipeg were affected, the communities of Grand Forks and East Grand Forks were virtually inundated. Flood water reached almost five kilometres inland, covering some homes to a depth of more than 15 metres. The total flood damage for the entire Red River region was in the order of US$3.5-billion.

While estimated to be only a once-in-100-years event, the 1997 flood came close to over-topping Winnipeg's existing flood protection infrastructure. The floodway protecting the city was designed to handle a flow of 60,000 cubic feet per second; the flow in 1997 peaked at 63,000 feet per second. To compensate, the province broke its own operational rules, which may have protected Winnipeg but caused more severe flooding downstream.

In the aftermath, the government of Manitoba responded with the Canada–Manitoba Partnership Agreement on Red River Valley Flood Protection, which resulted in a further $130-million being invested in additional upgrading of infrastructure in the Red River Valley, this time to minimize potential damage from future flood events of the magnitude of 1997. In combination with similar programs in the United States, the cost of reacting to the 1997 flood exceeded $4-billion. A floodway expansion project was later put forward by the

International Joint Commission which aimed to protect 450,000 people, 140,000 homes and 8,000 businesses from the risk of $12-billion in potential damages that could occur in the event of a once-in-700-year flood. The proposed cost of this program, to be funded equally by the federal and Manitoba governments, is estimated at $665-million.

Lake Agassiz again tried to recreate itself in 2009, in a flood which demonstrated that a number of vulnerabilities still existed in Manitoba's flood disaster plan, especially relating to severe ice conditions. Although only 2800 people were evacuated, many homes were accessible only by boat and 1000 square kilometres of farmland was submerged. A major Manitoba highway was closed for more than a month. Disaster assistance claims amounted to more than $40-million.

Then came the flood of 2011, which cost the province some $936-million, of which only $445-million is expected to be recovered from the federal government. In March 2012 Manitoba Finance Minister Stan Struthers announced that the province faced a budget deficit of almost $1-billion, more than double what had been expected. A special warrant for $297.2-million was approved by the provincial government to finance the shortfall, which was largely related to the flood of 2011. Neighbouring Saskatchewan and North Dakota together also had to absorb an additional $1-billion in costs associated with the 2011 disaster. Numbers like these suggest a direct link between hydrology and our economy.

The ghost of Lake Agassiz still haunts the Central Great Plains region, threatening to bankrupt it. In early 2013, four flooded First Nations communities around Lake Winnipeg filed a class action against the government of Manitoba for $950-million in damages. This made four lawsuits of this kind, totalling $1.3-billion, that have been brought as a result of the 2011 flood alone. What's more, the spring of 2013 was unusually cold, and snow lingered well into April. The prospect of two major floods in three years was not out of the question. Residents of the region are losing confidence in the capacity of their governments to protect them from hydro-climatic change.

Economic development is good but more is not always better: Boom and boomerang in the Central Great Plains

Many of the flood-related problems that exist presently in the Central Great Plains are a product of the region's own rapid economic success. The great legacy of the last Ice Age and glacial Lake Agassiz was the rich soils which, after European settlement, immediately made southern Manitoba one of the most productive agricultural regions in North America and one of the great breadbaskets of the world. Some 99 per cent of the region's natural prairie landscapes were made over to farming and other human uses. As prosperity grew globally, diets evolved to include more meat. The Central Great Plains responded by dramatically expanding livestock production. It was not long before Canada was not just famous for its wheat; it was also one of the top five pork and beef producers in the world.

As we've seen, however, this intensive agriculture – in tandem with large-scale land-use changes, altered hydrologic patterns and the annual spring floods – has resulted in nitrogen and phosphorus being flushed into Lake

Winnipeg in such volumes that it threatens to destroy the lake, which ultimately could wipe out the lake's $50-million-a-year fishing industry and seriously impact the province's $1.1-billion-a-year tourism industry. But Lake Winnipeg is only a symptom of a much greater problem. The damage caused by the persistent nutrient flushing from floods has now become so costly that it threatens to cancel out the economic gains produced by the agricultural boom in the region. Boom has become boomerang.

Why we can't keep up with flood disasters

No matter how many billions we spend on protection, we will not be able to keep up with the growing cost of flood damage in the Central Great Plains. Why? There are at least three reasons.

The first is that the design of dikes, canals, diversions and floodways has not adequately taken into account the extent to which accelerating changes in land use are altering the way surface waters move through the basin. It is estimated that as much as 90 per cent of the natural wetlands in southern Manitoba have now been drained.

By continuing to eradicate wetlands, farmers and other landowners collectively push expensive additions to regional flood protection systems to the limits of their design capacity. Current agricultural land-use policies, while conducive to improvements in production, are diametrically at odds with flood protection. The cost of the one is not being adequately accounted for in the cost of the other.

The second reason it has been impossible to keep up with the growing cost of flood damage in the Central Great Plains is that expanding human populations, intensification of agricultural production and resulting changes in land use have altered the hydrology of the region to such an extent that it has become increasingly vulnerable to more intense rainfall events of longer duration. Such rains result in much more surface water flowing over a landscape made much smoother by the removal of wetlands and thus more susceptible to flooding because of the reduced number of watercourses available to take up the increased flows. All of these problems are expected to get worse as mean temperatures throughout the region continue to rise. Warm air holds more water vapour than cold air does (see pages 62 and 65–66), which loads the dice for further flood events.

The third and biggest reason we can't keep up, however, relates not to agricultural practices or the need for more scientific knowledge or engineering finesse but to how we frame these manifold challenges and undertake to address them. We have yet to fully recognize the complex nature of the challenges we face. The current flooding situation has been largely characterized to date as a relatively straightforward environmental problem. While that may have been the reality at one time, it is no longer the case now. The deteriorating condition of Lake Winnipeg cannot be addressed unless it is seen as the broad, complexly intertwined issue it really is.

Avoiding an ecological endgame in the Central Great Plains

We have not been able to reduce the economic and social impacts associated with the deteriorating condition of Lake Winnipeg because we have not regarded the issue as anything more than a bounded, albeit complicated, problem affecting only one system within the larger network of jurisdictions that comprise the Central Great Plains region. Over time, however, the deterioration of this system has ramified into an ever more complex predicament that affects everyone who lives in or has economic ties to the basin. While persistent flooding is at its core an environmental issue, it now touches equally on matters related to the very structure of our society with respect to food security, the fundamental workings of our economy and the way we do politics within our democratic institutions, both here in North America and internationally. Proposed solutions to the flooding problem will not result in meaningful environmental restoration unless they reflect the elevated needs and aspirations of a better-informed society and are introduced and implemented at provincial, state, federal and international levels in a politically acceptable and efficient manner that does not threaten the existing economic fabric of the region.

Avoiding an endgame at Lake Winnipeg will not be a simple task. It can be accomplished, however, if we advance in the direction of enlightened water management practices that are already well established in the Central Great Plains. Much progress has been made, particularly in the past two decades. At one time it was thought that water should be managed solely within the confines of individual jurisdictions. Now we realize that water crosses all boundaries – natural, societal and political – over multiple scales of time.

It also used to be held that water systems were constrained by natural circumstances, and that cause and effect relationships were thoroughly understood and could be readily modelled. Now we know that water systems are actually part of a larger network comprised of both natural and societal elements that cross boundaries and change constantly, in ways that are not always predictable, in response to economic pressures and political choices.

We used to believe that decisions relating to the management of water should be made by experts; that scientific analysis had to precede public participation in decision-making; and that compromises were required from the outset in order to satisfy competing political demands. Now we realize that what happens to water is so important that all stakeholders and rights holders have to be involved at every decision-making step, including the initial framing of problems, and that monitoring and experimentation are critical elements in adaptive approaches that make greater resilience possible.

It used to be thought that hard bargaining on water issues was central to a zero-sum approach to what was considered effective water management. It was accepted that negotiations over allocation and use impacts inevitably created winners and losers. It is now seen that if we want to resolve complex problems, we must cultivate coalitional approaches that favour informed collaboration to arrive at effective non-zero-sum results. It is this approach that is most likely to produce solutions that will prevent the cost of managing floods from bankrupting the Central Great Plains and will avoid the irreversible decline of the health of Lake Winnipeg.

A scientific case for action

The mechanisms that are driving the greatest global ecological change are human population growth with attendant resource consumption, habitat transformation and fragmentation, energy production and consumption, and climate change. The rate of human population growth is now three orders of magnitude faster than it was when people first gathered together to form civilizations. Some 43 per cent of the surface of the earth is now taken up by food production. Much of the remaining landscapes have been occupied by cities or buried under roads.

It has been scientifically demonstrated that under continued stress biological systems can shift rapidly to a radically altered state. Abrupt ecological shifts lead to new mean conditions that are often outside the range observed in the previous state. It is projected that climates which contemporary life forms have never experienced could be prevalent over as much as 39 per cent of the globe within a century.

It is now known also that local-scale changes in ecological conditions can trigger changes in state over regions larger than the affected area. Tipping points in undisturbed areas have been found to occur when 50 to 90 per cent of the surrounding landscapes have been disturbed, as has occurred over the past century as agriculture transformed the prairies in both Canada and the United

States. In order to prevent irreversible damage to Lake Winnipeg and what might become a shift in the ecological state of the Central Great Plains of North America – or at least respond as best we can should these changes occur – it is necessary to address the root causes of human-induced landscape change in this region and improve our management of water and the ecosystem services that aquatic ecosystems provide.

It may be helpful to put the Lake Winnipeg circumstance into a larger hydro-climatic context. If you want to know what is happening to climate, pay attention to what is happening to water.

The first important effect water has on the global atmosphere relates, of course, to oceans. We are at last beginning to understand the profound influence of ocean currents on weather and climate. We are beginning to picture how the great circulation systems in both the Atlantic and the Pacific oscillate over decades and how these oscillations are reflected in cyclic changes in temperature and rainfall on each of the continents.

We are also beginning to understand the refrigerating influence of polar sea ice. Because the gradient in temperature between the poles and the tropics is what establishes many of our weather patterns, ice plays a critical role in modulating the temperature of the earth's atmosphere and its oceans. Polar ice is now seen as the thermostat that governs major weather patterns globally and regulates sea level. There isn't a person on the Great Plains or anywhere else on earth, therefore, who is not affected by how much ice there is at any given time and what it does to moderate our climate.

Because it responds so directly to warming temperatures, sea ice was on the agenda at the Convention of the Parties 18 organized by the UN Intergovernmental Panel on Climate Change in Doha, Qatar, in November 2012. The World Meteorological Organization reported there that ice cover in the Arctic between March and September that year had shrunk by 11.83 million square kilometres. In other words, the area of sea ice which melted that summer was nearly three million square kilometres larger than the entire landmass of Canada. The loss of Arctic sea ice and the diminution of the extent and duration of snowcover in the northern hemisphere are reducing the temperature gradient between the pole and the tropics, which appears to be altering the behaviour of the jet stream.

Jet streams are winds created as the planet spins inside the ragged blanket of its own atmosphere. These winds are fast flowing, relatively narrow currents that form at the boundaries of adjacent air masses that are significantly different in temperature, such as the polar region and the warmer air to the south. In a uniformly warmer and therefore more turbulent atmosphere, both warm and cold fronts now end up in places where they were not commonly found in the past. One of the reasons our weather appears to be all over the place is because it *is* all over the place. This is also one of the reasons why average temperatures don't give an accurate impression of what is happening to climate.

Shifts in temperature regimes are resulting in changes in the position of the thermal equator, which affects rainfall distribution. A weakened jet stream also appears to be resulting in high-pressure weather patterns sometimes lingering much longer than usual in the same region, creating heat waves. This may be one of the reasons why, in June of 2012, some 3000 temperature records were tied or broken in the United States alone.

New research indicates that the number of high-temperature weather events globally is increasing. James Hansen and company at NASA have demonstrated that between 1951 and 1980, extreme hot weather covered less than 1 per cent of the earth's surface at any given time. Now, extreme temperatures cover about 10 per cent of the global land area in summer. producing the kinds of heat waves experienced in Russia during the summer of 2010 and in parts of the US – Texas and Oklahoma in particular – in 2012. This trend persisted into the austral summer of 2012–13. Temperatures of such an extreme occurred in Australia in January 2013 that the Bureau of Meteorology famously added a new colour to the country's temperature maps, to represent the range 52 to 54°C. These hotter temperatures also demanded the creation of a new fire hazard index, to include a level beyond extreme which the Australians labelled "catastrophic."

Connecting the dots:
Canada's accelerating hydrologic cycle

Evidence that increasing temperatures are accelerating the manner and rate at which water is moving through the global hydrological cycle is now widely enough available that we can begin connecting the dots with respect to Canada's changing hydro-climatic conditions. Let us start in the North.

While we may not have perceived it as such, what is happening in the Arctic and throughout much of the Canadian boreal is exactly what is happening in much of the rest of the country. Our hydrology, which used to exhibit stationarity (see page 63), is now on the move. Water frozen in the form of ice, snow and permafrost is beginning to melt, and fresh water stored for thousands of years in cold lakes is beginning to evaporate. The water is not disappearing, however, There is as much of it on earth as there ever was; no more, no less. What is happening, though, is that warming is causing much of our water to change form and move to a different place in the hydrosphere, where it may not be available for our use when we want it. Warming is also concentrating more water as vapour in the atmosphere, from which it may suddenly re-emerge as liquid in volumes we haven't before experienced and don't have the means to easily manage. Similar hydrological changes are readily observable in Canada's western mountains.

Until recently, North American scientific attention has been focused on the rapid loss of glacier ice in Glacier National Park in the United States. In that park, 113 of the 150 glaciers that existed in 1860 have vanished. The reason for the attention was that the Americans actually knew what warming was doing to their ice. We here in Canada, however, had no idea of how rapidly our glaciers were disappearing. Now we do. Through the efforts of the research consortia IP3 (Improved Processes and Parameterization for Prediction in Cold Regions) and WC^{2}N (Western Canadian Cryospheric Network), researchers now know that we may have lost as many as 300 glaciers in the Canadian Rockies between 1920 and 2005. Dr. Garry Clarke of the University of British Columbia is one of this country's most respected glaciologists. His work, and that of his many colleagues, has demonstrated that our losses may be accelerating.

What is happening to our glaciers suggests that the future climate of the Canadian West may be very different than it is today. While glaciers may not be as important in terms of water total water supply as they once were, what is happening to glaciers may be a warning of other, far more significant threats. We already know that long before global warming has finished reducing the length and depth of our glaciers, it will already be after our mountain snowpack, and *that* could have a huge influence on our water supply.

Recent research outcomes provided by Dr. Danny Blair at the University of Winnipeg indicate that between 1979 and 2011 the rate of loss of June snowcover in the northern hemisphere has been in the order of 17.8 per cent per decade. What is troubling is that shrinkage in the extent and duration of snowcover in the mountain West will in fact become a feedback in its own right, further accelerating warming. While this will, of course, affect water supply on the prairies, nowhere will it be more immediately problematic than in the Columbia River basin.

Research findings based on the work of Dr. Alan Hamlet and the University of Washington's Climate Impacts Group project show that over the coming century the Columbia basin will change from being a snow-dominated hydrological cycle to one where winter rains prevail instead. While the northern, Canadian part of the Columbia basin is projected to lose little of its annual snowpack and snowcover by the middle of this century, the US portion could lose as much as 38 to 52 per cent of its winter snowpack. Overall precipitation may not diminish, but more of it is going to come as rain instead of snow. Similar model projections developed for the Sierra Nevada mountains in California demonstrate similar changes farther south. It appears the American West will be a very different place by mid-century. What is interesting, however, is how these changes are now seen to be linked with water levels in the Great Lakes and flooding in Toronto.

More dots connected: declining Great Lakes levels

At 59,600 square kilometres, Lake Huron is the second-largest of North America's Great Lakes. Only Lake Superior which is upstream, is larger. When measured at average annual low water, Lake Huron is estimated to hold 3540 cubic kilometres of water. The reason it is so large and contains so much water is that – like the glaciers of the Rockies – it is a landscape relic left behind from the last major glaciation. Despite its size, however, Lake Huron's level has diminished by 115 centimetres between 1997 and 2012, based on September averages.

While dredging of the St. Clair River outlet plays a role, it is thought that these falling lake levels are related in part to a diminished amount of precipitation falling as snow in winter over Lake Huron and Lake Superior. There has also been a decline in the extent and duration of ice on the lake in winter and a trend toward greater evaporation from hotter summer temperatures. Higher evaporation rates result in lower inflows into Lake Huron.

What we see from this is that the same warming that is causing glaciers and patterns of snow deposition to change in the West is also causing water left on the land after the last glaciation in the Great Lakes region to move to a different place in the hydrosphere. A rough calculation of the decline in level in Lake Huron alone suggests that as much as 67 cubic kilometres of water may have disappeared from this part of the Great Lakes system since 1997. So where is all this water going?

Still more dots: flooding in Toronto

One of the places the missing Great Lakes water is going is into the atmosphere, where it becomes available to fuel more frequent and intense extreme-weather events such as the one in 2005 that in only two hours caused some $700-million in flood damage to water infrastructure, roads and homes in Toronto. The city has had five once-in-100-years storms in the past 20 years. It has become very clear that rising temperatures and the increasing concentration of atmospheric water vapour are making what once were predictable natural events much worse. The algorithm upon which this assertion rests is called the Clausius–Clapeyron relation.

The Clausius–Clapeyron relation establishes that the amount of water the atmosphere can hold increases by about 7 per cent per degree Celsius, or about 4 per cent per degree Fahrenheit. The anticipated changes in precipitation inferred by the Clausius–Clapeyron equation are reasonably well simulated in global climate models. We are already seeing changes. Between 1948 and 2007 the mean temperature in Canada increased by 1.3°C. Canada is now also 12 per cent wetter on average than it was in the 1950s, and more frequent severe weather events are already a reality.

The Clausius–Clapeyron relation matters for another reason, too. Water vapour is a potent greenhouse gas in its own right. More water vapour in the atmosphere further increases the greenhouse effect. Thus a warmer atmosphere that holds more water becomes a climate feedback that in itself accelerates warming. So how are all of these events and changing circumstances connected?

The loss of hydrologic stationarity

To understand why additional human-caused climate warming is such a threat to established stability it is important to understand the central role water plays in our planet's weather and climate system. The fundamental threat that climate change poses relates to what hydrologists call stationarity.

Within the broader hydro-climatic context, stationarity is the notion that natural phenomena fluctuate within a fixed envelope of certainty which has permitted us a relatively high degree of confidence when it comes to predicting and managing the effects of weather and climate on our cities and our agriculture. This fixed envelope was something we created; it does not exist in nature, at least not for very long. Because of warmer atmospheric temperatures, however, whatever certainty stationarity provided no longer exists. This, we have recently discovered, is a lot more serious than we at first thought.

A US report entitled *Global Change and Extreme Hydrology: Testing Conventional Wisdom* (National Academies Press, 2011) confirms how serious the loss of hydrologic stationarity could be in North America and around the world if current trends persist. The findings of the National Academies analysis include consensus on the fact that anthropogenic land cover changes such as deforestation, wetland destruction, urban expansion, dams, irrigation projects and other water diversions have significant impact on the duration and intensity of floods and droughts. The report concludes that "continuing to use the assumption of stationarity in designing water management systems is, in fact, no longer practical or even defensible."

The old math and the old methods no longer work. What's more, Canada and the US are not the only countries confronted by such changes and it looks as if we may have a lot more company in the future.

For example, scientific attention focused on atmospheric dynamics related to climate warming has revealed some very interesting phenomena that confirm the Clausius–Clapeyron relationship. In 1990 about 500,000 cubic kilometres of water went through the global hydrological cycle each year. Conservative estimates at the time projected that warming would result in an additional 25,000 cubic kilometres of water circulating through the entire earth system. We are beginning to understand now where that extra water is going and what these changes may mean in the future. Suddenly we are aware of rare storm phenomena such as the *derecho* (deh-REY-cho) which have always existed but have suddenly leapt into public consciousness because of the damage their intensity and increasing frequency are causing in the eastern United States. These are not ordinary summer thunderstorms. They are widespread, long-lived windstorm events that cause straight-line swaths of destruction 400 kilometres across. The extent of damage these storms cause inland is similar to that from hurricanes in coastal areas.

Researchers have also discovered the presence of what are being called atmospheric rivers. Atmospheric rivers have probably always existed, but now with satellites we can identify them. Research meteorologist F. Martin Ralph describes these rivers as narrow, transient corridors of strong water vapour transport in mid-latitude winter storms. Centred about a kilometre above sea level, these corridors of intense winds and moist air can be 400–500 kilometres across and thousands of kilometres long. They can carry the equivalent of 7 to 15 times the average daily discharge of the Mississippi River.

Atmospheric rivers may well have been around for eternity, but now they are overflowing their cloud banks in ways we have never witnessed before, producing floods of the enormous magnitude we saw in Australia and Pakistan in 2010. As we have seen, the effects of widespread flooding are not contained within national borders but can affect food and commodity prices globally. Here we encounter the complicated nexus where water, climate and food production meet, and sometimes collide head-on.

Why is this relevant to Lake Winnipeg? It is

possible that the atmospheric river phenomenon may have contributed to major flooding in parts of the Central Great Plains region of North America in 2011. It was this flooding that drew attention to the fact that here was a region in plain sight, right in the centre of North America, that may be changing as quickly as the Arctic. It appeared that the flooding was evidence that the Central Great Plains were approaching – perhaps had already passed over – an invisible threshold into a new hydro-climatic state which many residents were unable to even cope with, let alone adapt to.

Damage from such events is already on the rise, which will cause insurance rates to increase and a greater proportion of taxes to be committed to infrastructure protection and disaster relief. The fear is that the cost of this ongoing damage may over time be substantial enough in some places to make it difficult to sustain prosperity as we know it today and still keep our cities, towns, national transportation systems and other crucial infra-structure in functional repair. The fear is that southern Manitoba and the Central Great Plains as a whole may be one of those places.

We have yet to react to the loss of hydrologic stationarity. We do not as yet have an adequate replacement for stationarity statistics. The National Academies report observes that agencies responsible for managing extreme weather events have been provided with only marginally useful scientific information about the likely effects of future climate on the hydrologic cycle. The report argues that the era in which field monitoring stations could be discontinued based on stationary statistical assumptions is over. In a non-stationary world, expanded basic monitoring of key elements of the hydrologic cycle is essential to support analyses of hydrologic extremes with any confidence.

The report argues that there is not enough interaction or adequate knowledge exchange among climate scientists, water scientists, engineers and other professionals to address the challenges associated with loss of stationarity. The report also argues that we have to figure out how we intend to manage hydrologic extremes, with or without scientific certainty. As we have seen in Manitoba and the Central Great Plains as a whole, there is real urgency in this.

Some further consequences
of hydro-climatic change

It is not just water that is affected by hydro-climatic change. Warming atmospheric temperatures in combination with increases in mean water temperatures are generating companion impacts that are beginning to cascade through every aquatic and terrestrial ecosystem in the country. The loss of ecological stationarity begins at the molecular level and radiates all through the cellular, bacterial and fungal domains, which have largely been held in check in Canada by the effect of cold temperatures on water.

Invasive species

There are perhaps 8.66 trillion kilograms of insects alive at any given time all over the globe. A companion loss of biological stationarity brought about by warmer winter temperatures over much of southern Canada will allow colonization by insects from more southern climes. Whole systems and the species that compose them will be on the move in response to warming water temperatures on one hand and to what happens at the other end of the scale when the $-40°C$ thermal barrier falls. This will exacerbate the existing problem of invasive species.

There are some 182 known invasive species in the Great Lakes, mostly introduced through discarded ballast water of ocean-going freighters. While the initial onslaught may have been stemmed, popular boating lakes have become vectors from which invasive species are advancing westward. Zebra mussels, for example, have crossed the continent from the Great Lakes to California. It may be only a matter of time before this problem can be added to those the region is already trying to address.

These are the visible, surface effects of the loss of fundamental hydrological predictability and certainty in Canada and globally. Now let's look at some cultural aspects.

Cultural and legal implications
Might an energized global water cycle have linguistic, legal and liability implications? The loss of hydrologic stationarity will certainly affect language, because it will in some cases dramatically modify what words mean. How will it tinge the connotation of "normal," "mean" or "average"?

What will words like "risk" and "security" come to mean? Barbara Kingsolver's latest novel, *Flight Behaviour*, is evidence that literature has already begun to track these new directions.

Certainly the loss of hydrologic stability will affect our laws, if only because the changes that are occurring affect liability – that is to say, who is responsible for protecting whom from what. Sadly, as we have seen with flooding, it could all come down to which parties we blame. Precedents in tort law in the US make it increasingly clear that it may not be long before politicians and members of the professions can be held legally accountable if, in ignoring climate change threats, their policies, decisions or solutions cause undue or unnecessary harm to others.

Matters in dispute include building codes and design standards; development approvals and restrictions; and negligence in disclosure in all manner of areas, including real estate transactions and business contracts. Even the timeliness and effectiveness of adaptation initiatives may face legal liability challenges. In 2010 alone more than 120 lawsuits of this kind were filed. While not as yet ruled on in the courts, these actions are seen as a harbinger of the kinds of legal challenges we can expect in a more hydro-climatically charged world.

Insurance in a higher-risk world

As mentioned in chapter 1, the insurance industry has recognized for some time that the world has changed in terms of the increased frequency and duration of extreme weather events. As one senior analyst put it in 2012, "Climate risk liability is no longer unthinkable, and it is not even an emerging risk. It has within a very short period of time become a 'risk iceberg,' a real hazard of which only a minor part is visible..."

The problem is that we do not as yet have an adequate replacement for stationarity statistics. Until we find a new way of substantiating appropriate action in the absence of stationarity, risks will become increasingly difficult to predict or to price, not just in Winnipeg or Regina, Fargo or Moorhead, but everywhere.

This situation is so serious that the insurance sector is threatening not to provide coverage to those municipalities that do not adequately manage, maintain and upgrade their infrastructure. What is already clear also is that people living in places where extreme weather events recur are now finding it more expensive to buy insurance, if they can get coverage at all. More people, therefore, are relying on their governments to provide disaster relief.

Private insurance, however, is a different form of risk management than government disaster relief. With commercial insurance, policyholders pay into a pool of money that becomes large enough to cover the cost of catastrophic events. When the inevitable happens, the payout is more or less automatic and the losses are absorbed by the pool, not by individual interests. Governments, on the other hand, are self-insured. When a disaster occurs, governments that are not running fiscal surpluses have to borrow to manage the crisis immediately and deal with the debt later.

In places affected by regularly recurring extreme weather events, economic growth will be difficult. Regions like the Central Great Plains may be lucky to hang on to the prosperity they have. For economies already on the edge, the increased frequency of extreme weather events could be what pushes them into insolvency. The flooding in Athens in economically troubled Greece that took place in February of 2013 is a case in point. The threat in all this, however, is not just to public and private material wealth but also to valuable and irreplaceable ecosystem services. How do you insure those?

The whole other issue of sea level rise aside, damage from extreme weather events is already causing insurance rates to climb. And not everyone is insured or can afford to be. As we saw during the flooding that occurred in the Central Great Plains region in 2011, uninsured losses can be eight to ten times greater than those covered by insurance.

Governance

The lesson we learn from all this is that the loss of hydrologic stationarity has the potential to cause a great deal of human misery and suffering, even in the developed world. Those on – or driven to – the margins will suffer the most; and their problems, as we have seen in Manitoba, will have legal consequences for governments at all levels. It has been proposed that, in the complicated and unpredictable realm of politics, governance in a hydrologically destabilized world may require new kinds of leaders, and that we ought to begin cultivating those kinds of leaders now.

A Region in Trouble: The Central Great Plains

At first it was thought this region so affected by hydro-climatic change could be defined and confined geographically as the Lake Winnipeg basin. Though we later found out that the problem was actually much larger than that, it does radiate outward from Lake Winnipeg.

Like many prairie lakes, Lake Winnipeg was likely moderately contaminated by nutrients even in its natural state. This is because of the presence of phosphorus-rich soils in the western and southern parts of the lake's catchment. Big changes have occurred since the 1990s, however, because of a combination of factors which include changes to the physical characteristics of the watershed. Flows in the Saskatchewan part of the system have declined because rising temperatures have caused greater reservoir evaporation and irrigators have been abstracting more water. Meanwhile, flows in the Red and Winnipeg river basins have grown because of destruction of wetlands and increased stream channelization. These larger flows have been accompanied by more "nutrient loading" brought about by significant expansion in livestock operations. The term "nutrient loading" in this context can be misleading, however, as was noted by the Manitoba Minister of Conservation and Water Stewardship, the Hon. Gordon Mackintosh, at the annual Lake of the Woods Water Quality Forum, in May 2013. "My mother," he said, "taught me that nutrients were good for you. Well, the nutrients going into Lake Winnipeg are not good for you." Minister Mackintosh is correct. What is pouring into Lake Winnipeg can hardly be called nutrients, and they certainly aren't good for you. The main sources of these so-called nutrients are agricultural manure, fertilizer and pesticide runoff as well as municipal and private sewage sources.* Despite the relatively sparse human population, the total excrement load – animal plus human – in the Lake Winnipeg basin within Manitoba has been estimated to be equivalent to that of a human population of nearly 50 million. This

* It is interesting that the agriculture industry in North America has managed to have the contaminants produced by agricultural runoff be identified in the public imagination as "nutrients." In 2010 *National Geographic* published a book edited by Irena Saline entitled *Written in Water: Messages of Hope for Earth's Most Precious Resource.* One essay in the book, "The Unmentionables," by Rose George, observes that we should see past euphemisms to understand what sanitation really means. A large part of what is pouring into and contaminating Lake Winnipeg and many other water bodies in the Central Great Plains is fecal matter. George observes that 1 gram (0.035 ounces) of feces can contain 10 million viruses, 1 million bacteria, 1,000 parasite cysts and 100 worm eggs. "Public health professionals talk about water-borne diseases," George observes, "but that is a euphemism for the truth. These are shit-related diseases."

nutrient loading is in addition to the already extensive use of synthetic fertilizers. Between 1994 and 2007 inclusive, phosphorus inputs into Lake Winnipeg increased by 71 per cent, or 5.1 per cent per year.

The first evidence of problems in the basin became evident when algal blooms in Lake Winnipeg began to grow in size over the course of each summer. Algal abundance has increased by 300 to 500 per cent since 1900. Blooms of up to 15,000 square kilometres have now begun to appear in the lake annually. When these blooms begin to die and decompose, oxygen is consumed and the resulting decline in available oxygen threatens aquatic life. Lake Winnipeg, with its high mid-summer chlorophyll loads, is now considered one of the most eutrophic of the world's great lakes. But there is also another problem.

The proportion of Lake Winnipeg phytoplankton that is cyanobacteria rose from 56 per cent in 1969 to over 80 per cent in 2012. The concentration of toxic, nitrogen-fixing cyanobacteria has increased by 1000 per cent since 1990. Some species of cyanobacteria create toxins called microcystins. In controlled experiments, microcystins have been shown to cause liver hemorrhage and promote tumour development in mammals. They have also been implicated in illnesses and deaths of domestic animals, wildlife and humans. It is now held that the increased area of algal blooms and the growing presence of toxic cyanobacteria in Lake Winnipeg are a warning of accelerating eco-hydrological changes, not just in the immediate Lake Winnipeg area but throughout the Central Great Plains.

Dr. John Pomeroy and his colleagues at the University of Saskatchewan have observed an increase in rainfall on the Canadian prairies. More of that precipitation, however, is occurring in multi-day rainfall events generated by frontal storms coming, for example, from the Gulf of Mexico, as opposed to shorter-term, localized convective rainfall. This change clearly affects water quality. Pomeroy et al. have recorded a 10,000-fold increase in the mobilization of fecal coliforms during these multi-day events as compared to the mobilization that typically occurs during localized thunderstorms. Increases in the intensity and duration of extreme weather events that appear to be becoming the norm are likely to further increase nutrient input into the Lake Winnipeg system.

Spring flooding throughout the region has also been increasing in the past decade, setting new records. The floods of 2011 cost Manitoba a billion dollars. It is an interesting coincidence that this amount is equal to the fiscal deficit of the provincial government the following year, which, as mentioned earlier, suggests a direct link between ecology and economy. Combined flood damage in neighbouring North Dakota and Saskatchewan were in the same range. So what is happening here?

Land use: climate change without greenhouse gases
In the heat of contemporary debate we sometimes forget that human activities can cause climate change even in the absence of greenhouse gas emissions. Like many climate change circumstances that have occurred in humanity's past, the problems we face in the Central Great Plains are, first and foremost, ecological in origin. In order to increase agricultural productivity, we have changed the prairie landscape dramatically. These changes naturally have had implications for

how water moves on the land. Because local clay soils are hard to work when wet, and the growing season in the region is short, up to 90 per cent of natural wetlands throughout the region were drained. These wetlands not only stored water in times of flood but were sinks in which nitrogen and phosphorus concentrated, allowing natural ecosystem function to purify runoff before it poured into Lake Winnipeg.

There is no mystery about what is happening. More frequent and intense spring floods flush nitrogen and phosphorus contained in livestock and wildlife feces and agricultural fertilizers from the land surface into watercourses that flow into Lake Winnipeg. The ultra-high concentrations of these substances form the nutrient supply for the algal blooms.

Because civilizations in places like the Middle East and China, which flourished long before fossil fuels came into existence, learned the consequences of sweeping land-use changes the hard way, we can predict what happens next. Ecological change elicits hydrological change which elicits climate change. In our time, however, we are learning that if, on top of all these effects, you add into the atmosphere more of certain substances that already compose it – such as carbon dioxide and methane – then eco-hydro-climatic change accelerates. That appears to be what may be happening now in the Central Great Plains region of North America.

Cascading effects from land-use changes elsewhere in the Canadian West

Because a province like Alberta forms the upper headwater reaches of the Lake Winnipeg basin, we can see how eco-hydro-climatic change is affecting the broader West by examining what has happened over time upstream. Since Alberta became a province in 1905 its landscape has been completely altered.

Cumulative effects researcher Dr. Brad Stelfox has demonstrated that in just over a century, in Alberta alone, we have turned 11 million hectares of the Great Plains into cultivated cropland. We have transformed 14 million hectares into livestock grazing lands and 24.2 million hectares of forests into Forest Management Areas. We have paved 225,000 hectares under cities and towns. Another 340,000 hectares has been transformed into rural residential areas, or what are called "acreages." An additional 1.1 million hectares has been used by the energy sector for seismic lines, well sites, pipelines and processing plants. Our roads and railways occupy another 400,000 hectares, and 30,000 hectares more has been sacrificed for recreation. In only four generations of development, total human activity in the province now accounts for 50 million hectares. Much of the most intensive part of this activity takes place in the Central Great Plains region, and more than 90 per cent of the landscapes of the Canadian Prairies have been altered from their original pristine condition.

This land use is not passive. As Dr. Stelfox has pointed out, "Alberta is definitely firing on all land-use cylinders." Each year, it produces up to 2 million head of cattle; 3 million head of swine; 120 million kilograms of poultry; 35 million tonnes of field crops; 25 million cubic metres of timber; 160 million cubic metres of natural gas; 35 million cubic metres of conventional oil; 80 million cubic metres of bitumen; 35 million tonnes of coal; and between 1200 and 1500 petajoules of electricity.

It will come as no surprise to anyone that such massive land-use changes, combined with resource extraction on this scale, are having an impact on the province's water. Alberta's growing water woes include diminished surface water flows, particularly in small streams and ponds, and smaller main-stem river flow and aquifer volume, all of which are reflected in the deterioration of water quality.

Finally, the situation we must adapt to is climatic, because if you alter the land and its hydrology, its climate invariably changes too. Few Albertans realize the extent to which their climate has already been affected by global warming in and of itself. That will come as winter and spring temperatures continue to rise. It is becoming very difficult, however, to ignore the combined, simultaneous effects of early but rapid, accelerating and in many cases irreversible eco-hydro-climatic change.

As Dr. John Pomeroy's work on the Smith Creek basin demonstrates, the same kind of eco-hydro-climatic change that is happening in Alberta is also occurring in Saskatchewan, largely as a result of similar large-scale land-use changes and the destruction of natural wetlands. We have also discovered that the reason why the South Saskatchewan River doesn't contribute significantly to eutrophication in Lake Winnipeg is that 90 per cent of the huge phosphorus load it carries gets trapped in the reservoir behind the Lake Diefenbaker dam. But even though Lake Diefenbaker is very large, all you have to do is look at Lake Winnipeg to see where this is going.

As neighbouring Manitoba, Minnesota and North Dakota have been no less transformed in terms of land use, these impacts accumulate and multiply as you move downstream through the basin toward Canada's sixth-largest body of fresh water.

The worsening flood problem

But something else is now happening as well. As we move toward the centre of the continent, we should not be surprised to observe that eco-hydro-climatic change is already being compounded by more extreme weather events of the intensity and duration predicted by climate models. We should expect the risks to increase. Because of the reduction in natural storage of water and the loss of stationarity, it is anticipated that extreme weather events causing flooding will increase in frequency and duration over time. If natural storage remains limited, it will be at full capacity more of the year, which means that even small storms will trigger much larger events.

In the Fargo–Moorhead area, astride the boundary between North Dakota and Minnesota, there has been a measurable increase in large floods since 1969 and especially since 1995. Based on the Army Corps of Engineers' new hydrological models, the 2009 flood at Fargo, the largest on record, is now considered less than a once-in-a-century event. The inundation of North Dakota in 2011 further demonstrated the greater frequency and larger volumes of flooding that characterize what appears to be a new and energized hydro-climatic regime.

Now, most climate models project that warming in the Central Great Plains will be in the order of 5 to 8°C by the end of the century. And while there is still a great deal we don't know about the atmosphere, it is conceivable that given this projected warming, and if the Clausius–Clapeyron relation applies, as much as 35 to 56 per cent more atmospheric moisture could be available for storm events in the region. Thus what used to be once-in-100-years events will happen much more frequently, and truly catastrophic floods will not be uncommon. Such events could have a staggering effect on the economy of the region. It has been estimated, for example, that a once-in-500-year flood event in the US portion of the Red River basin could – depending on the time of year – cause between $10-billion and $15-billion in damage. The cost of mitigating this by restoring up to 20 per cent of lost water-storage capacity is estimated to be at least $1.5-billion in the American portion of the Red River basin alone. The cost of adapting infrastructure to these changes is estimated at $4.6-billion for the US portion of the basin.

So, can the damage being done to Lake Winnipeg be reversed? The answer is yes, but the scale of such a project should not be underestimated. Highly eutrophied lakes have been restored to their former health, but it is costly and it takes time. Lakes that have recovered from eutrophication following the control of phosphorus inputs include Lakes 226, 261, 303 and 304 in the Experimental Lakes Area in northwestern Ontario. Partial recovery has also been achieved in Lake Erie and Lake Ontario in Canada and in Moses Lake and Lake Washington in Washington state. Five large lakes in Sweden have been brought back from the brink. Lago Maggiore in Italy and Lake Balaton in Hungary have also been restored, as have Lakes Geneva, Zurich and Lucerne in Switzerland.

Because Lake Constance, also in Switzerland, recovered despite the tendency of a warmer climate to make the lake more productive, it is probably the most cited example of how eutrophication can be brought under control. Lake Constance became eutrophied as a result of nutrient-contaminated inflows, and it took €2-billion, or about $2.6-billion, and 40 years to bring it back to its original condition.

Lake Winnipeg is 45 times the size of Lake Constance.

I predicted in 2004 that if nothing meaningful was done, the scale of the Lake Winnipeg problem would eventually attract international attention. Unfortunately this has happened and the attention is far from positive.

In February 2013 Lake Winnipeg was identified by the Global Nature Fund as the world's "Threatened Lake of the Year," based on the rate of its deterioration. When the news reached Canada, many thought the prospect was improbable. Yet I personally have seen lakes in China that look like green jelly, and lakes damaged to that extent cannot be restored within any time frame meaningful to anyone alive today. The Global Nature Fund judges were of the opinion that the rate and geographical extent of the eco-hydro-climatic changes causing the eutrophication of Lake Winnipeg were unparalleled anywhere else in the world. This new notoriety is not something Canadians should take lightly, either. It is the first time in history that a developed country in a temperate region has earned this dubious distinction.

The most common question asked about this disgraceful designation is what will happen to Lake Winnipeg if we don't do anything about the threats to its health. My answer is that many very committed people are already trying to do something about the problem. A better question might be: What will happen to Lake Winnipeg if we don't do enough, quickly enough, to reverse its deterioration? We have been candy-coating the answer to that question for 20 years, and as a result not enough has been done to address the problem. The unsweetened answer is that if we don't get going on the restoration of Lake Winnipeg, Manitobans may be doomed to live next to one of the largest open-air sewers in the world. I doubt they would stand for that. The dubious Global Nature Fund distinction does suggest, however, that we need to recognize – as the rest of the world has – that it is time to get serious about saving Lake Winnipeg.

A key point that needs to be made is that it is not just Manitoba and Canada that deserve a black eye as a result of Lake Winnipeg "winning" this unfortunate international recognition. The fact remains that Lake Winnipeg is a symbol of a much larger problem. Cyanobacteria are among the oldest known photosynthetic micro-organisms. Their long evolutionary history has enabled them to survive enormous changes in the earth's climate for 3½ billion years. We now have evidence from around the world which makes it clear that harmful cyanobacteria take full ad-vantage of human-caused eutrophication caused by nutrient over-enrichment, excessive water withdrawals and reservoir construction. Rising temperatures are already resulting in enhanced vertical stratification of aquatic ecosystems and changes in climate that very much favour cyano-bacteria blooms in eutrophic waters.

Recent research by Diane Orihel of the University of Alberta and her colleagues reported that the cyanobacterial toxin microcystin has now been detected in 246 water bodies across Canada, at levels exceeding maximum guidelines in every province. Some 18 per cent of the samples in 41 per cent of lakes exceed World Health Organization standards. While lakes in Alberta are in particularly serious condition, problems exist right across the country. The presence of these toxins is now an issue of national health and environmental concern.

Though not specifically stated in the Orihel study, it may fairly be inferred that microcystins are likely to become ever more present in Canadian lakes as water temperatures rise in response to mean air temperature increases and as agricultural activity is intensified in response to the need to feed rapidly growing human populations.

Finding our way to a new normal

We need to recognize that the problems we presently face in the Central Great Plains are a lot more serious than we previously thought. The loss of hydrologic stationarity is a significant issue because it means our hydrology is on the move and we are not sure where it will stop or even whether we will ever be able to expect stability again. For those who live in the region, adaptation to the loss of hydrologic stationarity will be one of the greatest challenges of this generation. In order to sustain its economy and provide hope for the future, the Central Great Plains may have to be re-engineered from a hydrological perspective. This may be the only way we can protect the Manitoba economy and secure the globally important agricultural future of the West. It may also be the only way Lake Winnipeg can be saved. We have to realize as well that what is happening here could ultimately happen elsewhere and have an effect throughout the entire North American West.

So what more do we need to do?

The first thing is to recognize and accept that – for all our efforts and good intentions – what we are doing now is not enough to solve the problem. Yes, consensus has been reached on important dimensions of the issue. Many important steps have been taken and a number of very successful programs have been developed. But we are not getting far enough fast enough.

It is time to face the situation squarely: What do you do when the consensus you have reached is too limited in scope and action and does not fully engage all the interests necessary to adequately address the problem? What do you do when despite your very best efforts the problem is still getting worse and in fact looks like it might be getting away on you altogether?

To address this threat, we have to understand that the magnitude of the problem is of a different order than we have ever experienced before. What we have to realize is that the loss of hydrologic stationarity is a societal game changer. Please allow me to repeat that. *What we have to realize is that the loss of hydrologic stationarity is a societal game changer.* What has become clear is that it isn't just emissions cuts that we need to achieve to restore climatic stability. Difficult as those may be, they will not be enough. In order to adapt and flourish we have to set new ecological restoration goals as well.

To achieve sustainability, to save our invaluable agricultural sector and salvage Lake Winnipeg along the way, nothing less will be required than a complete re-engineering of the eco-hydrology of the entire Central Great Plains region.

The situation is far from hopeless

All this said, the sky is not falling and the world is not coming to an end. There is no place nor is there a need for desperate, paralyzed resignation. With the "Northern Voices, Northern Waters" water stewardship strategy, the government of the Northwest Territories and its Aboriginal and federal government partners have demonstrated that there is nothing in the Canadian federal–provincial political structure that makes it impossible to undertake the kinds of wide-ranging water policy reform that are necessary to adapt successfully to climate change. With the NWT example before us, it is no longer possible to say that such levels of reform are out of the question because of legislative, legal, policy or political obstacles. We can do it. This should be taken as really good news. Governments don't have to be limited to playing around at the edges of reform. They can make real change happen. Sustainability, therefore, is not an impossible goal.

The people of the Central Great Plains are not without means. They know that true adaptation is not just survival but a commitment to flourishing in a changed world. Some 76 per cent of all natural disasters globally are not earthquakes or volcanoes; they are hydrological events. The most effective way to adapt quickly to the growing number of negative consequences and costly feedbacks associated with rapid eco-hydro-climatic change is to manage water more effectively.

We know what to do. We have leading-edge water treatment technology and – for the moment at least – we can afford to employ it. We know how to restore ecosystem function, and cooperation exists at provincial and state levels in the basin to make such restoration possible. Others in Europe and elsewhere have been where we are now and we can learn from them. If we decide to do so, we could even pay farmers and other agricultural producers to sustain certain ecological processes that will slow or moderate climate change effects while at the same time protecting the agricultural future of the region.

In order to orchestrate the actions of millions of people in four provinces and four states, we need to remobilize at a higher and more inte-grated level. A wide range of interests in the basin appear ready to do just this. And it is interesting to note that the drivers behind this impetus are not only the established environmental organizations but the Manitoba Chambers of

Commerce and the International Red River Basin Commission as well. For the first time, it is the larger economic community that is bringing this issue before government as an urgent priority – and many others are helping them. What is missing is an organizing force that will bring all of these interests together and synergize their efforts both on the ground and politically. But that too may be coming.

It is important to build on what we already know works. Collaborative initiatives that involve all sectors, such as the educational program called LakeFriendly.ca, work very well, but they have to be expanded to include the entire basin. Sooner or later, elements of such programs will have to become mandatory rather than voluntary.

The parameters of massive, long-term flood management measures such as those presently being undertaken in the US part of the Red River Basin must be adopted in Canada. They must also be expanded to ensure they really do address concerns related to nutrient transport as it ultimately affects the ecological condition of Lake Winnipeg. Until lidar data becomes available for Canadian parts of the basin, Canada cannot be a serious player in advanced continental flood management or nutrient control.

It has been determined that wetlands are among the most productive and economically valuable ecosystems in the world. Unfortunately, over half of the wetland ecosystems that existed in North America, Europe, Australia and China in the early 20th century have been destroyed. An analysis of 621 wetland sites around the world demonstrates that even a century of restoration efforts, biological structure and biochemical function remain on average 26 per cent and 23 per cent lower respectively than in undisturbed wetlands. Given current rates of wetland degradation, established methods of restoration will not slow loss of wetland ecosystem function globally.

Ducks Unlimited's Dr. Pascal Badiou reported at the Red Zone III community forum in 2012 that destruction of remaining natural wetlands on the Canadian prairies continues to occur ten times faster than the restoration rate. What's more, even where restoration is undertaken, it creates wetlands that perform barely half the ecosystem functioning of the original sites. It may be time to consider paying farmers, other agricultural producers and landowners for protecting and sustaining important ecosystem services such as those provided by wetlands.

While it could be viewed as a "tailpipe" solution that doesn't get to the heart of the problem of nutrient loading of the basin's streams and rivers, ideas like the International Institute of Sustainable Development's bio-economy concept are worth exploring, not just for their own sake but for the potential they may lead to in the future. Far more immediately important, however, is fertilizer and manure management. In a sense, we have to protect our crucial agricultural sector from its own excesses. Tough choices have to be made about agricultural practices such as whether or not new regulations are necessary for intensive livestock operations and whether use of synthetic fertilizers should be limited or no longer permitted in certain circumstances.

None of these solutions, however, can be promoted as adequate in itself. We have to recognize that each year we waste on piecemeal approaches to the Lake Winnipeg problem likely adds one, two, even three or more years to the decades that will be required to restore the lake to some semblance of its original condition, if indeed warming temperatures will permit us to do so.

The gravity of this problem has to be fully acknowledged. No one in this basin should be excused from helping. We need some important interests to step up to the plate. We need to involve the broader economic community, which includes Big Agriculture and various interests in the financial, insurance and philanthropic communities as well as scientists and First Nations in both countries, in an effort to raise the kind of awareness and level of funding that will ensure that those working now and in the future on the Lake Winnipeg problem have the resources they need to be successful.

Can we save Lake Winnipeg? Of course we can. There is still room to move if we want to achieve that goal. But we would be well advised – all of us – to get moving now while that room still exists.

Toward a New Water Ethic in Canada

In the middle of the first decade of the 21st century the government of Canada decided that our country's principal means of responding to the growing global climate threat would be through activities and programs aimed at increasing our adaptability to changing climatic conditions, whatever they may be. The words "adaptation" and "resilience" made a grand entry into the popular Canadian vocabulary.

However, the pace at which we have actually moved in the direction of fulfilling these intentions has been painfully slow. For all my genuine desire to be positive and helpful in my capacity as an adviser to a number of climate change adaptation initiatives at both the national and regional levels, I am not sure we are really doing anything meaningful at all. At the time of this writing at least, it appears we are engaged in little more than polite talk. Even in places where we are really trying, our best efforts are being mocked and overshadowed by relentless population and economic growth, expanding land-use effects and ever-increasing emissions. Except in coastal areas where there is a clear threat of sea level rise, there seems to be a general sense that nothing is going to happen that is going to be that much out of the ordinary. Yes, it may be a little bit warmer and the weather may be a little more unpredictable but we will be able to deal with it.

At a more regional scale, the situation is at once better and in some ways worse. Adaptation has been taken up earnestly as a cause in many parts of Canada by a generation of young community leaders who have gravitated toward such issues. The problem, however, as pointed out in chapter 1, is that powerful forces of denial have so contaminated the climate change debate in so many places that the subject cannot even be brought up in public discourse except obliquely. We have also allowed those same interests to employ sophisticated public relations tactics to carefully control and define the language that can and cannot be used in the discussion. To a very large extent, these tactics have allowed interests that favour the status quo to frame the rules of engagement in all public discourse related to the climate issues.

In some places, particularly in Western Canada, concerned people are reluctant to even engage directly in discussion of water-related climate impacts for fear of hostile push-back from climate change deniers. They are reduced to referring to weather when they mean climate and to increasing resilience when they mean adaptation. Some have been so intimidated by anti-climate-change interests that they have started to operate under euphemisms which, while palatable at some level of public discourse, completely subvert and undermine understanding of the fundamental reality of what climate change could mean to our society's future. One of the few things that appears to have the force required to rock us out of our complacency and overcome our meek acceptance that the economy is somehow more important than the ecology from which it is derived is the changing state of Canadian waters.

Does Canada face a water crisis? Absolutely,

yes, but it is not one we might have expected. While supply and quality issues plague many parts of the country, the real water crisis facing Canada is the loss of hydrologic stability that has resulted from wholesale changes in land use and a combination of natural and human-caused climate change. I have used the Central Great Plains region of the continent as this country's most dramatic example of that loss of stability, but other areas – the Arctic, certainly, as well as the northern boreal, the Great Lakes, all three of Canada's coasts and the mountain West – could all be facing similar or related problems as rising temperatures further accelerate the global hydrological cycle.

Remarkably, the realization is emerging, in both scientific research and the economic circles with which that research overlaps, that we are now in fact looking at what in time could very well become the beginnings of a national climate adaptation emergency. Under less serious circumstances, adaptation might have required only relatively superficial changes to patterns of our collective behaviour. Unfortunately, the prospect of radical and irreversible eco-hydro-climatic change suggests we likely face extraordinary circumstances that will demand that we re-examine our most fundamental beliefs. That re-evaluation could and should begin with a thorough reassessment of how we value water in this country – and how we ought to regard and manage this most precious of Canada's liquid assets in the future. The immediate challenge for this generation is to save Lake Winnipeg. Unfortunately, in doing so we may have to rethink our relationship between where and how we live, which may mean re-examining what it really means to be a Canadian in an era of accelerating ecological, hydrological and climatic change.

Evidence that denial is a lie, by year of publication

The End of Nature, Bill McKibben, New York: Random House, 1989.

Boiling Point: How Politicians, Big Oil and Coal, Journalists and Activists Are Fuelling the Climate Crisis, Ross Gelbspan, New York: Basic Books, 2004.

Red Sky at Morning: America and the Crisis of the Global Environment, James Gustave Speth, New Haven, Conn.: Yale University Press, 2004.

The Ethics of Climate Change: Right and Wrong in a Warming World, James Garvey, New York: Continuum, 2008.

Storms of My Grandchildren: The Truth about the Coming Climate Catastrophe and Our Last Chance To Save Humanity, James Hansen, New York: Bloomsbury Press, 2009.

Merchants of Doubt: How a Handful of Scientists Obscured the Truth on Issues from Tobacco Smoke to Global Warming, Naomi Oreskes and Erik M. Conway, New York: Bloomsbury Press, 2010.

Eaarth: Making a Life on a Tough New Planet, Bill McKibben, Toronto: Knopf Canada, 2010.

Denying Science: Conspiracy Theories, Media Distortions and the War against Reality, John Grant, Amherst, NY: Prometheus Books, 2011.

The Inquisition of Climate Science, James Lawrence Powell, New York: Columbia University Press, 2011.

The Hockey Stick and the Climate Wars: Dispatches from the Front Lines, Michael E. Mann, New York: Columbia University Press, 2012.

www.deathofevidence.ca

www.desmogblog.com

www.desmog.ca

www.evidencefordemocracy.ca

www.scienceuncensored.ca

Other Titles in this Series

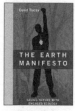

The Earth Manifesto

Saving Nature with Engaged Ecology

David Tracey

ISBN 978-1-927330-89-0

The Homeward Wolf

Kevin Van Tighem

ISBN 978-1-927330-83-8

On Fracking

C. Alexia Lane

ISBN 978-1-927330-80-7

Little Black Lies

Corporate and Political Spin in the Global War for Oil

Jeff Gailus

ISBN 978-1-926855-68-4

Digging the City

An Urban Agriculture Manifesto

Rhona McAdam

ISBN 978-1-927330-21-0

Gift Ecology

Reimagining a Sustainable World

Peter Denton

ISBN 978-1-927330-40-1

The Insatiable Bark Beetle

Dr. Reese Halter

ISBN 978-1-926855-67-7

The Incomparable Honeybee

and the Economics of Pollination Revised & Updated

Dr. Reese Halter

ISBN 978-1-926855-65-3

The Beaver Manifesto

Glynnis Hood

ISBN 978-1-926855-58-5

The Grizzly Manifesto

In Defence of the Great Bear

Jeff Gailus

ISBN 978-1-897522-83-7

Becoming Water

Glaciers in a Warming World

Mike Demuth

ISBN 978-1-926855-72-1

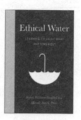

Ethical Water

Learning To Value What Matters Most

Robert William Sandford & Merrell-Ann S. Phare

ISBN 978-1-926855-70-7

Denying the Source

The Crisis of First Nations Water Rights

Merrell-Ann S. Phare

ISBN 978-1-897522-61-5

The Weekender Effect

Hyperdevelopment in Mountain Towns

Robert William Sandford

ISBN 978-1-897522-10-3

RMB saved the following resources by printing the
pages of this book on chlorine-free paper made with
100% post-consumer waste:

Trees · 7, fully grown
Water · 3,107 gallons
Energy · 3 million BTUs
Solid Waste · 208 pounds
Greenhouse Gases · 573 pounds

CALCULATIONS BASED ON RESEARCH BY ENVIRONMENTAL DEFENSE AND
THE PAPER TASK FORCE. MANUFACTURED AT FRIESENS CORPORATION.